THRIVING AT 50+

THRIVING AT 50+

THE 7 PRINCIPLES TO REINVENT AND REBRAND YOURSELF

WENDY MARX

NEW DEGREE PRESS

THRIVING AT 50+
The 7 Principles to Reinvent and Rebrand Yourself

ISBN

978-1-64137-603-7   *Paperback*

978-1-64137-605-1   *Kindle Ebook*

978-1-64137-607-5   *Digital Ebook*

To George—for traveling with me on my journey
and never letting go.

Reinvent your life because you must;
it is your life and its history and the
present belong only to you.

−CHARLES BUKOWSKI

CONTENTS

The 7 Principles to
REINVENT AND REBRAND
Yourself at 50+

Having a Growth Mindset

People who successfully reinvent themselves are adept at trying something new and unafraid of failing. They imbibe a growth mindset.

Being Uncomfortable

To reinvent yourself, you need to embrace the paradox of being comfortable enough with being uncomfortable to take risks.

Willingness to Learn

The path of reinvention is often crooked with zigs and zags as you try new things. You'll need to make mistakes to learn and grow.

Finding Your Purpose

To find your purpose, you must claim your own life, which often gets lost in the day-to-day shuffle. Your life purpose is about discovering what's most important to you.

Storytelling

Stories are a lifeline during your reinvention process, providing emotional ballast to support you. They reassure you that your plans make sense. Similarly, they are the narrative of your life you share with others.

Personal Branding

Think of personal branding as subtraction and addition. First you scrape away the excess—what's no longer relevant or what's holding you back.

Social Media / Mentoring

Key to getting any reinvention to fly are catalysts, such as social media and mentoring. Think of them as the propeller to your reinvention—what helps it soar.

PREFACE

Nicolas Babin thought his life was over at age forty-nine.

Walking home from work, the technology executive was hit by a speeding car. His right knee was busted, and he lost his sense of smell, taste, and hearing in his left ear. His spirit was crushed as he sank into despair.

"I realized I was not the same man," Babin told me.

The former Nicolas Babin was robust and athletic. In his thirty-year career, he had achieved a number of firsts, including commercializing the world's first GPS system and AI robot, both at Sony.

Babin thought about giving up. He didn't want to return to the hectic pace of his old job as director of digital transformation and business development at the global company Neopost. Considering he suffered from post-traumatic stress disorder after the accident, returning to his office, which was near the scene of the accident, would have been intolerable.

But when people began seeking his advice on technology problems, he had an aha moment. He realized the old Nicolas Babin still had value. Just as he did for Sony, he rebranded himself, this time as a digital transformation consultant.

Today, Babin Business Consulting is a thriving company with clients worldwide. Ironically, Babin is now happy the car accident disrupted his plans. It gave him the impetus to reinvent himself at a later stage in life.

Nicolas Babin's story offers a happy ending to horrific circumstances. But is his story unique? Can ordinary people who have trod the same well-worn work path for years reinvent and rebrand themselves? It's easy to think that at a certain point in life, your career journey is set. You are who you are. How can you teach an old dog new tricks? Don't you have to pack up your career in at 50+ or at least slide downward to the finish line?

NEGATIVE STEREOTYPES

Negative perceptions of older workers abound. One persistent idea is that baby boomers are standing in the way of younger talent moving up in an organization. In Deloitte's Global Human Capital Trends Report, 15 percent of respondents believed that older employees were "an impediment to rising talent."[1]

---

1   Dimple Agarwal, et al., "The Longevity Dividend: Work in an Era of 100-Year Lives."

While it's easy to believe that millennials are replacing boomers in the US workplace, statistics tell a different story. Recent research from the US Department of Labor shows that by 2024, one in four US workers will be fifty-five or older. To put this in context, in 1994, workers over fifty-five represented about one in ten workers.[2]

As boomers hurdle through competing challenges of supporting families and saving enough for a longer lifespan, they can't afford to stop working. Only 24 percent of today's US workers age fifty-five and older have saved more than $250,000 (excluding homes and pensions), according to Deloitte[3]

With the surge of boomers working, I wanted to study how people like Nicolas Babin and those in other walks of life and careers were able to reinvent themselves around age fifty or older, a time when ageism rears its head. What I found has changed my own mindset about reinvention and rebranding. I learned that it isn't necessarily easy or fast. But it's possible. And, done correctly, it can transform your life.

THE BRAND CALLED YOU
My interest in reinvention didn't begin with Babin. I first became excited by reinvention and personal branding in 1997 when I read an article by Tom Peters, famous for his book *In Search of Excellence*, called "The Brand Called You."

---

2   Jeff Schwartz, Steve Hatfield, Kelly Monahan, and Siri Anderson, "No Time to Retire: Redesigning Work for Our Aging Workforce."
3   Ibid.

A manifesto for personal branding, Peters called for readers to brand themselves as a product, "Brand You." The article had my name on it.

I had reinvented and rebranded myself multiple times. Peters made me realize that my career restlessness and swerves, while perhaps extreme, were examples of the power of reinvention and personal branding. I had successfully migrated from social work to journalism to marketing to PR, rebranding myself along the way. With this book, I am on my fifth reinvention as a coach for people over fifty seeking their next act.

A recruiter once shrugged me off as a career-changer. After that, I artfully cut some of my experience from my resumé so I looked more straight-arrow. Today, I proudly own my history.

Beyond my own experience, I have spent some twenty-five years rebranding the clients of my B2B PR agency. As part of our public relations initiatives, we have helped rebrand and reposition our clients and their companies and developed their thought-leadership bona fides. As our virtually unknown clients would move from anonymity to industry icon, the strength of branding became evident.

Writing this book is part of my journey and process. As a baby boomer myself, I know that it gets tougher to reinvent yourself the older you are. You may not be as flexible or tech-savvy as your millennial cousins, but it is possible. And now I understand how.

THE 50+ PARADOX

People over fifty are in a unique position. On the one hand, they are armed with life experience and savvy; on the other hand, the typical workplace doesn't value that experience and knowledge. Often, older workers aren't familiar with the current lingo and the latest technology gizmos; however, they have emotional intelligence and leadership skills in spades. Age discrimination is still rampant. Almost seventeen thousand age discrimination complaints were filed with The Equal Employment Opportunity Commission in 2018.[4]

Despite the challenges, those most successful in reinventing and rebranding themselves have buffed up their strengths and shored up or compensated for any weaknesses. They have developed a process and strategy that underpins their efforts. This book will propose a framework you can use to thrive in your next act—regardless of what it is.

THE SEVEN PRINCIPLES OF REINVENTION AND REBRANDING

You'll discover seven principles of reinvention and rebranding told through the stories of people over fifty from all backgrounds and professions. The principles presented sequentially will give you the tools to reinvent and rebrand yourself at your job, in a new business, or in a new career or lifestyle.

---

4   "EEOC Releases Fiscal Year 2018 Enforcement and Litigation Data."

The principles are based on my interviews with people who have successfully reinvented themselves and those still struggling to do so. They also come from my own personal experience reinventing myself multiple times and my research into the psychology of reinvention and personal branding. They are not just theoretical but practical steps you can take now.

The seven chapters correspond to the principles, and each includes an interactive portion called "Your Turn," so you can apply the principles to your life. And to ensure your success, the book includes a resource guide with templates to assist you in applying the book's lessons.

This book is for anyone over fifty trying and needing to determine his or her next act. You could be a 50+ person laid off and needing to find another job or livelihood. Or you might want to change careers or start a new business or way of life. I use the term 50+ loosely throughout. Truly, anyone wanting to revitalize his or her career and life will find the book helpful. In fact, if you start thinking with a rebranding and reinvention mindset at age forty, you will be that much better served when you need to start a new act at age fifty.

You'll learn about people like Sree Sreenivasan, who knows more about digital technology than many millennials, because of his years teaching social media at Columbia University and serving as the chief digital officer of New York City and the Metropolitan Museum of Art. Yet even Sreenivasan has run up against ageism as he reinvented himself as a digital consultant. I share his strategies for dealing with ageism and reinvention.

You'll hear the story of Rita G. (she asked that I not use her full name), who has said it has taken her two years to feel better since her layoff from her thirty-year career in higher education administration. You'll learn how she recovered as she gave herself time to breathe and reinvented herself as a therapist and learning coach.

You'll also learn about Mitchell Levy, who reached the heights of consulting, speaking, and teaching, becoming informally known as Mr. Ecommerce, only to see it wash away in the dot-com bust of 2002. Using a framework model, Levy has reinvented himself several times since, first as a book publisher and now as a CEO of a ghostwriting publishing firm. Today, he's happier than he's ever been.

In the end, the seven principles of reinvention and personal branding will do more than help you build a new act. You'll gain greater control of your life and be in a better place than you ever thought possible. You won't be looking back with nostalgia but ahead with gusto.

HOW TO READ THIS BOOK

This book is for people in every stage of reinvention. You may be toying with the idea or just getting your feet wet. Or you could be further along in the process. For that reason, you may want to personalize how you read this book.

The introduction provides an overview of reinvention and its challenges and opportunities. The next seven chapters are each devoted to one principle. While written sequentially, each can stand alone. If you want to bone up on personal branding, don't hesitate to start with that chapter. Or if you want to understand the concept of "failing fast," read Chapter 3: Willingness to Learn.

Feel free to skip around so you get what you need. There's no pressure to read from start to finish, but of course you may do so. You can also begin with the "Your Turn" sections at the end of each chapter, which includes questions to help you move further along on your own reinvention journey. Make sure to explore the resource guide at the book's conclusion, which includes a self-assessment and branding exercise, among other items.

Remember that while the book has a theoretical framework and seven principles, it's meant to be enjoyable to read—and practical. Don't consider it a threatening schoolmarm but a helpful coach tapping you on the shoulder and encouraging you on your own journey. Bon voyage.

REINVENTION

———

"You can get what you want, or you can just get old."

—BILLY JOEL

In a wonderful *Seinfeld* episode, George Costanza loses his job and is deciding what to do next. In inimitable George fashion, he thinks he can do anything.

How about a general manager for a sports club? How about a talk show host? Or why not a movie projectionist? After all, he likes to watch movies, and so what if he can't run a projector?

It's humorous because it's ludicrous. Yet it's how some people imagine career reinvention. You might as well ask a genie to transform you. Voilà, and a ready market of people emerge, eager to snap up what you're selling. But reinvention isn't magic. It takes work, introspection, digging deep, searching wide—and it doesn't happen overnight.

The greatest misconception people have about being 50+ and wanting to reinvent themselves is thinking that it's binary. It's either abracadabra simple, as George thought in the *Seinfeld* episode, or it's unattainable. In the latter, you're skulking around with a scarlet *A* branded on your face—for *aged*. The Kleenex has piled up for a giant pity party.

Actually, reinvention for those who are 50+ lies somewhere in the middle of these two extremes. Yes, it's difficult and takes time. It can be frustrating, even diabolical, given age discrimination and a possible need to take a lower-paying job temporarily to survive while you're reinventing yourself. But with the right strategy and attitude, it's possible. This book will show you how.

* * *

By reinvention, I'm not talking about a 50+-year-old suddenly becoming a prize fighter or another dramatic transformation. While those shape-shiftings sometimes happen, most reinventions are what Marc Freedman, CEO and president of Encore.org, an organization tapping into the wisdom of people over fifty, calls "reintegration, not reinvention." It's people "crafting a new idea that's deeply rooted in earlier chapters and activities," Freedman wrote.[5] It's molding what you've been into something a little different.

"People often think that reinvention requires a total change in their lives," said John Tarnoff, reinvention career coach

---

5   Marc Freedman, "The Dangerous Myth of Reinvention."

and author. "Instead, it may be doubling down on whatever you are already doing and reinventing your career from the inside out. . . . It might also be something more radical, like taking a reduction in salary to better position yourself for a more satisfying or strategic role."[6]

While you don't need to entirely change your spots, reinvention can benefit from thoughtful, artful editing. Like a great work of art, what you erase and replace can bring your canvas to life. I am using the word *reinvention* to mean the creation of a life that's relevant, meaningful, and purposeful—whether that involves a major change or tweaking. It doesn't emerge out of thin air but builds on your past, as you'll see in the upcoming chapters.

As the poet Charles Bukowski wrote,

"Reinvent your life because you must;
it is your life and its history and the present
belong only to you."[7]

THE CHALLENGES OF BEING OVER FIFTY
Being 50+ in America is a little like being an immigrant in your own country. You don't speak millennial, you aren't viewing a video while watching TV, texting friends, and

---

6   Kerry Hannon, "The Key to Career Success After 50."
7   From Charles Bukowski, "The Pleasures of the Damned."

Instagramming. You aren't flaunting tattoos or your toned body. Technology isn't as natural to you as breathing. You're unlikely to know what *skip meetings, cadence calls,* and *huddles* mean, noted leadership experts Elizabeth and Lisa Earle McLeod.[8] Moreover, you're often a target of discrimination, or particularly, if you're an older woman—invisible. And to top it off, if you want to retire, you may not have the wherewithal to do so.

Prior to 2009, most Americans planned to retire before age sixty-five. Since then, most say they will retire after age sixty-five.[9] The Great Recession of 2007–2009 curtailed many people's retirement plans, according to the US Equal Employment Opportunity Commission. More than 10.5 million Americans over sixty-five are working, more than at any other time since the end of the century and more than 1.5 times the number working in 2000, according to the US Bureau of Labor Statistics. And nearly two-thirds are working full-time compared to a little over half working full-time in 2000.[10]

AARP research shows that finances are the main reason boomers say they plan to work into retirement. The financial crunch isn't difficult to decipher. Only twenty-four

---

8   Elizabeth McLeod and Lisa Earle McLeod, "The Hidden Challenge to Getting Hired When You're Over 50 —And How to Overcome It."

9   Frank Newport, "Snapshot: Average American Predicts Retirement Age of 66."

10 Victoria A. Lipnic, "The State of Age Discrimination and Older Workers in the U.S. 50 Years After the Age Discrimination in Employment Act (ADEA)."

percent of today's US workers over fifty-five have saved more than $250,000 (excluding homes and pensions), according to Deloitte.[11]

Unfortunately, finding work at 50+ can take all your reserves. Companies are not holding casting calls for the 50+. You may be forced to settle for a less desirable job, accept lower wages than you need, and be unemployed longer than someone younger. If you're fifty-five or older, you're likely looking at waiting twenty-seven weeks or more to find work.

And it's a crucible moment if your only job choice offers no health insurance or retirement benefits. About twenty percent of workers age fifty to sixty-two fall into that class, according to the Center for Retirement Research at Boston College.

"They're probably low-paid," said Alicia Munnell, director of the center. "Some have erratic schedules."[12] All of these financial issues don't make it easy. And societal attitudes about aging make it worse.

As you age, a many-headed beast rears its head, blocking workplace doors. If you've been rejected for a job by someone half your age and told you're not a good fit, you may well have confronted the beast—ageism.

---

11 Jeff Schwartz, et al. "No Time to Retire: Redesigning Work for Our Aging Workforce."
12 Paula Span, "Your Uber Driver Is 'Retired'? You Shouldn't Be Surprised."

While age discrimination is illegal, proving it is another story. Lori A. Trawinski, director of banking and finance at AARP's Public Policy Institute, nailed it. "Ageism is one of the last isms that still seem acceptable in our society," she said at Inclusion in Design 2019, a conference for empowering older women. She noted that while sixty-four percent of global CEOs have a diversity and inclusion program, only eight percent include age in their program.

"Today it is socially unacceptable to ignore, ridicule, or stereotype someone based on their gender, race, or sexual orientation," said Jo Ann Jenkins, the CEO of AARP. "So why is it still acceptable to do this to people based on their age?"[13] Realistically, life at 50+ can be challenging with the dual threats of ageism and finances.

THE UNRETIREMENT YEARS
Adding to the stress is the financial burden that can accompany longevity. At age fifty, you face another two or three decades to support yourself, needing more financial resources, especially if your health deteriorates or you're facing a chronic illness. Yet we draw a blank when imagining our "unretirement years."

Stanford University longevity expert Laura Carstensen frequently asks people, "If you had thirty extra years in your life, where would you put them?" No one, she said, ever suggested

---

13   Paul Irving, "When No One Retires."

adding the thirty years to old age. Yet, she said, "This is precisely what we've done."[14]

Consequently, many assumptions about aging are wrong, according to Carstensen, at a time when you aren't ready to be put out to pasture. In fact, some aspects of life improve as we get older. "Emotional well-being gets better as people get older," said Carstensen. "Our stores of knowledge go up, and in the last fifty years, every birth cohort that has arrived at sixty-five has been healthier than the one before."

In fact, sometimes you're your own worst enemy and miss what's hiding in plain sight—the many positives underneath the challenges of being 50+. As Susan Chadick, CEO of Chadick Advisors, a transition advisory firm for people shifting to another field, reminded me, "People over fifty, especially women, have the interpersonal understanding to suss out a situation and understand how it will play out. People over fifty know how to build coalitions, promote other people's ideas, because they already have the wisdom and don't have to prove anything all over again. They have the ability to mentor and to bridge the generation gap."

"Today, turning fifty no longer marks the beginning of a long, slow descent into old age; instead, it marks the beginning of a new period of growth, an extended middle age that did not exist for most of our ancestors," wrote AARP's Jenkins in *Disrupt Aging: A Bold New Path to Living Your Best Life at Every Age.* "It's a time when people start embracing the idea of living longer,

---

14 "Let's Retire Retirement."

living better, and maintaining a balanced, vital lifestyle."[15] In other words, it's time to welcome a reinvention.

It's helpful to think of reinvention as a spectrum. At one end are people needing to work for finances or for health insurance, and where tweaking a few skills is enough to keep their job or obtain another. Moving along the spectrum are people starting their own businesses, taking part-time jobs, or entering a new field. This may require learning new skills or retooling for another industry. At the far end are people not needing extra income but seeking more purpose in their lives—whether through work, hobbies, or volunteering.

These reinvention scenarios aren't mutually exclusive. For example, someone needing a job may also want to find more purpose or meaning in life. Your place on the spectrum will likely change over time. Initially, you may need to learn a few skills and later want to move into a new field or stop working entirely. What doesn't change is that at 50+ you may be looking at thirty additional years. How are you going to find new ways to live with purpose and meaning?

As in attaining any goal, reinvention doesn't happen in a vacuum. The key to any successful reinvention is looking inward and recognizing your accomplishments.

"People often think that to reinvent themselves, they need to get rid of everything they've done instead of figuring out how

---

15 Jo Ann Jenkins with Boe Workman, "Disrupt Aging: A Bold New Path to Living Your Best Life."

to incorporate that into their brand, which actually makes them more valuable," said Marie Zimenoff, CEO of Career

Thought Leaders and Resumé Writing Academy. "The value of what you've done is going to be the story of your value moving forward."

ADOPTING AN IMMIGRANT ATTITUDE

What can you do at 50+ to be empowered and effective? Foremost, you must arm yourself to be better fortified to meet the monster of ageism. Let's return to the analogy of an immigrant but do so from a position of strength.

For this, let's enlist the help of Sree Sreenivasan, a leading consultant, speaker, and trainer for nonprofits, corporations, start-ups, and executives, who at age nine immigrated to New York City from Russia (his father was an Indian diplomat) and whose parents are Indian. Sreenivasan said that his immigrant experience gave him a leg up at age forty-nine as he was marketing his wares as a consultant. Just as he did as an immigrant, he worked hard and was on top of his game.

Even Sreenivasan with his tough hide, however, ran up against the dog whistle of ageism. Sreenivasan, who knows more about digital technology than many millennials, said he interviewed several years ago with a progressive company with the most woke people. Yet the millennials he interviewed with didn't know how to use him.

"They didn't think I could help them, when in fact I could. I had the benefit of being Mr. Digital and Mr. Social," he said. "And even then, I experienced ageism."

People couldn't understand what a forty-six-year-old could do for the digital world.

"There's no magical number where the issue starts," he said. "It's not like they love you at forty-eight and then at fifty are reluctant to hire you. It's not like some magic thing that happens at forty-five or fifty."

Surprisingly, those wielding the ageism cudgel can be any age, even old themselves.

"The older people think it's always safer to hire younger people, and the young people don't know what older people can do," Sreenivasan said. "They also see high dollar signs on an older person's back without realizing the value the older person brings."

Sreenivasan said his experience teaching and supervising younger people in his digital workshops and classes has helped him counter the question of what he can offer. You probably don't have Sreenivasan's teaching experience. But you can benefit from his immigrant and minority experience.

"Most minorities and immigrants have to be doubly prepared and work harder to make it through life in America," he said. Similarly, those of us over fifty need to adopt an immigrant mentality. "You need to be well versed in what's happening, what's new," he advised. Resting on your laurels is not an option if you want to create a new act.

Frankly, it's easy to be smug about your achievements and think someone should be lucky to hire you with your years of experience. But being dismissive of technology and millennials and reveling in your old accomplishments won't get you far. Instead, advised Sreenivasan, say, "This is what I know. This is what I don't know. I am committed to learning. I will teach and coach and help."

Kerry Hannon, the author of *Great Jobs for Everyone 50+* and *Never Too Old to Get Rich: The Entrepreneur's Guide to Starting a Business Mid-Life*, shared with me wise advice for combating ageism.

"Be on top of your game," Hannon said. "Make sure you have done everything you can to keep up with technology and changes in your field. Market your age as a plus. Workers fifty and up tend to be self-starters, know how to get the job done, and don't need as much hand-holding as those with less experience. A great benefit to being older is that you have a good deal of knowledge and leadership ability."

In addition, Hannon acknowledged that part of ageism is stereotyping based on appearance. To counter that, she urged, "Be physically fit. Interviewers will judge a book by its cover, even if it is subliminal. An older worker who is physically fit exudes a get-up-and-go attitude. People want to work with you. . . . I don't mean you have to run a fast mile. You just need to be in shape. . . . You're selling the entire package of who you are—not just your work experience and talent." The powerful lesson is that you have the tools to overcome ageism.

"Reinvention after fifty is more than possible," wrote Dorie Clark, adjunct professor at Duke University's Fuqua School of Business and the author of *Reinventing You.* "It's critical to keeping your skills fresh and your work fulfilling. Between staying current with social media, owning your history, reconnecting with old contacts, and shaking up the ossified view that current colleagues may have of you, you'll soon be ready for the next chapter in your professional life."[16]

In the succeeding chapters, allow yourself to be vulnerable as you're sorting things out. You'll acquire a road map and path forward for your reinvention. And you'll learn how, in Clark's words, "to normalize reinvention."

Reinvention has its own language and attitude that frees you from the harmful stereotypes of old age. If you're told you can't have a meaningful, purposeful life, you may internalize that. By embracing a different mindset and vocabulary, you'll develop a new way to engage and empower yourself. Let's discover how to do so in the next chapter: having a growth mindset.

---

16   Dorie Clark, "How to Reinvent Yourself After 50."

YOUR TURN

Where are you on your reinvention timeline? Just thinking about it? Halfway through it? Plot where you are and where you want to be. Draw a graph with one line saying *goals*, the other representing *skills* you need to acquire and *people* to network with to help you get there. This will be your initial reinvention map to help you move ahead.

CHAPTER 1

HAVING A GROWTH MINDSET

"People today want to collaborate only with people who will assure them what they're doing is right. What they need to do instead is collaborate with people who will challenge them."

−RAY STASIECZKO, FOUNDER OF TEASRA,

THE INNOVATION CHANNEL

A few years ago, I attended a fiftieth high school reunion with an old friend. I didn't go to the high school (my family had moved), but I wanted to reconnect with some elementary school friends who were to attend. To my surprise, people who had been slackers or easy to write off in elementary school had carved out impressive careers. One boy, the proverbial troublemaker who never seemed very bright, had become a distinguished physician and professor. Another, who had been quiet and unremarkable, had written multiple books and had an illustrious marketing career. And yet another classmate who had been as smart as a whip in school, while successful, didn't grow into a standout, running a company or the country.

What happened? Was I so wrong in my assessments?

Stanford University psychologist Carol S. Dweck has spent years researching the concept of mindset and how it influences behavior. She distinguishes between a fixed and a growth mindset. Those with a fixed mindset are rigidity connoisseurs, stuck in one place.

"A fixed mindset is when people believe their basic qualities— their intelligence, their talents, their abilities—are just fixed traits. They have a certain amount, and that's that," Dweck said in an interview in *Harvard Business Review.*[17]

On the other hand, people with a growth mindset embrace change. "They believe that even basic talents and abilities can be developed over time through experience, mentorship, and so on," Dweck said. "And these are the people who go for it. They're not always worried about how smart they are, how they'll look, what a mistake will mean. They challenge themselves and grow."[18]

---

17   Sarah Green, "The Right Mindset for Success."
18   Ibid.

It's not that the people who were stars when young suddenly got less smart or talented. According to Dweck, they "may have believed all the hype, the idea that they just have it. And they become afraid of making mistakes. They become afraid of tarnishing their image. And because they're fearful of venturing out of their comfort zone, they don't take the risks or develop the abilities they're capable of." Meanwhile, people you didn't think would succeed aren't hemmed in by their self-perceptions. "These people maybe didn't have an image to uphold, didn't feel the weight of other people's expectations, and just followed their passions and developed their abilities," said Dweck.[19]

Dweck's research provides a useful framework for examining career reinvention. If you believe that you can't change, that your talents are fixed, your self-talk becomes a self-fulfilling prophecy. You don't or won't grow and change. In fact, as you age, it becomes harder to escape the stereotypes besetting older people. You are flooded with images that getting older means becoming slower, less able to learn new things. It's the cartoon image of the doddering old aunt or uncle.

And unfortunately, ageism is pervasive. Facebook's Mark Zuckerberg in 2007 famously told an audience at Stanford, "I want to stress the importance of being young and technical. Young people are just smarter."[20] Zuckerberg's statement is notorious for its bluntness, but the notion is commonplace. As Kathy Gottberg, author and wellness expert, said in an interview

---

19 Ibid.
20 Preston Gralla, "Old And In The Way."

on The Senior List website, "The number one problem in our country that plagues people as they grow older is the perception that once you reach a certain age, it is all downhill."[21]

Kim Norton Butler, a clinical psychologist turned full-time mom who transformed herself into a storytelling consultant after writing *Story: The Art of Standing Out*, told me, "I think that age is a vulnerability if you make it one. If you don't make it one, I think you can work around it. But some work needs to be done. Ask yourself, 'How am I different than someone who's twenty? What do I bring to the table? And what are my strengths?' And I think it's important to bring your parenting experience and make that a marketable skill. Because it definitely gives you people skills and soft skills."

If you believe that you can't change, that your talents are fixed, your self-talk becomes a self-fulfilling prophecy. You don't or won't grow and change.

A SELF-FULFILLING PROPHECY

Author and editor Richard Eisenberg, on the website Next Avenue, wrote about the challenges of midlife employees based on presentations by two retirement experts. In his article, he discussed how easy it is to get sideswiped by stereotypes and start internalizing

---

21   Amie Clark, "Expert Interview Series: Kathy Gottberg: Aging, And Living A Fulfilling Life."

employers' negative perception. Drawing on the insights of corporate trainer and adjunct professor Gillian Leithman, Eisenberg pointed out that people often think, "Maybe I am old and I can't learn anything new. Maybe my time has passed."[22]

Instead, Leithman and her co-presenter, life and retirement transition coach, therapist, and author Dorian Mintzer, recommended that older people adopt a "new courageous mindset. Try new things. Get curious,"[23] said Leithman. This very much relates to Dweck's growth mindset.

In her book, *Mindset: The New Psychology of Success*, Dweck wrote, "After thirty years, my research has shown that the *view* you adopt for yourself profoundly affects the way you lead your life. It can determine whether you become the person you want to be and whether you accomplish the things you value."[24]

Dorie Clark, a career reinvention expert, professor, author, and speaker, told me that older people can be blindsided by perceptions. While people sometimes subscribe to "stereotypes about older professionals not being as good at technology or being somewhat outdated," Clark said, workers over fifty should not "get too hung up on it, because that is the kind of belief that can become a spiral." Instead, she advised, "Make sure you are taking pains to demonstrate proactively that you are current, that your ideas are fresh, that you're keeping up, that you did not stop learning in 1985."

---

22   Richard Eisenberg, "New Mindset for Midlife Employees."
23   Ibid.
24   Carol S. Dweck, Mindset: *The New Psychology of Success.* (6)

People with a growth mindset, while not Pollyannaish about aging, are hooked on its potential for change. *Peanuts* cartoonist Charles Schulz once commented about getting old, "Just remember, once you are over the hill, you begin to pick up speed." Or as entrepreneur, author, and speaker Gary Vaynerchuk said in a YouTube video, "What blows me away is how many of you have decided you're finished. The fact that you didn't do it in your twenties, thirties, or forties actually means nothing. Psst—you have a lot more time than you think."[25]

Of course, reinvention is far from a walk in the park. You don't just snap your fingers and reinvent yourself at age fifty—though you might long for the reinvention genie to answer your wishes.

Career coach and author John Tarnoff, in an interview in *Forbes*, explained how challenging reinvention can be. He was struck by the difficulty people have when they "make a shift to something new. They have a mindset that is so attached to the old job, the old career. I'm hearing how emotionally challenging it is for people who are very, very willing otherwise and interested and committed to changing their lives." They must deal with an emotional toll, he added, "that comes from all the years they have been working with a company, the people, the place, the culture—all of the trappings of their identity are so wrapped up in the past."

Reinvention can be a high-wire act. In Marc Freedman's book, *The Big Shift: Navigating the New Stage Beyond Midlife*, he told the story of Meredith McKenzie, who reinvented herself

---

25   Gary Vaynerchuk, "A Note to My 50 Year Old Self."

after her husband died and she suffered a serious accident. Her reinvention trajectory wasn't smooth and involved setbacks before she could satisfy her passion for river protection and restoration while supporting herself. She described her reinvention as "walking the high trapeze without a net."[26] Letting go of your old self-image is a scary process.

THE RELUCTANT RELICS

Being tied to your old identity is one end of a chain that can slow your reinvention. The other is resting on your laurels. After all, at 50+ you've worked hard to get where you are. Why do you need to change? Isn't it time for your Hollywood ending? That fixed mindset, however, only hobbles you.

As personal branding speaker and author William Arruda told me, a fixed mindset says "'You know what, I've been really successful. I haven't really worried about branding myself. I'm not online. I don't even have a LinkedIn account. And I've achieved this certain level of success. Why should I start thinking about this now?'" To correct this, Arruda added, "A major mindset shift has to happen."

> Being tied to your old identity is one end of a chain that can slow your reinvention. The other is resting on your laurels.

26   Marc Freedman, *The Big Shift: Navigating the New Stage Beyond Midlife. (25)*

Arruda used a pithy image to describe what occurs if you don't change, saying you become a "reluctant relic." He explained that "if you don't overtly build your brand, if you achieved a level of success and haven't really thought about it and haven't done anything to demonstrate that you're still a player, then you're going to have the brand of a kind of relic. And that's one of the reasons people who are 50+ have to work doubly hard to get past the mindset and to make sure that other people see them as really relevant, as people they want to know."

Keith Keller, who at age fifty-four had reinvented himself multiple times, including becoming a Twitter phenomenon, said he gets a lot of guff from baby boomers over what he does. They tell him, "'I grew up in an age before computers. I don't need any of this app thing, this phone thing, this laptop thing. I don't want to do any of that. I just want to go down to the caff, have a beer with my mates, have lunch, and talk to real people in a room.' No worries," he told me. "If you want to do that, that's fine. There's plenty of room for the natural, organic, friendly community stuff. A whole life could be lived there. But that's not the life I want."

While Keller tips the scales on fearlessness, his attitude is echoed to some degree in all the people I've interviewed for this book who have successfully reinvented themselves. These effective shape-shifters are adept at trying something new and unafraid of failing. They imbibe a growth mindset.

Ray Stasieczko, a managed print services expert, has reinvented himself multiple times, fearless of trying something new or "looking stupid" doing it. At age fifty-nine, he's creating a twenty-minute online show.

"I'll put the show on YouTube and then share it through LinkedIn, where I'll be able to interview people from the copying industry. I'll do it in my own candid way," he told me. "Most of the business information is too canned. Professional. Some executive stands in front of a piece of equipment. People watch the video for five seconds and turn it off."

Stasieczko's business videos were anything but boring. "With me," he said, people will think, "'Ray's gonna mispronounce the word, Ray's gonna say something so outrageous that people are gonna be shocked.' Or, you know, 'Ray's gonna call out this competitor on a problem or tell the copying industry what could be stupid.'"

"When you look in the same place everyone else is looking, you miss the same thing everyone else was missing," Stasieczko said, quoting R. Keith Sawyer in *Group Genius: The Creative Power of Collaboration.*

Bear in mind that you don't want to leave your reinvention to chance. If you wait for lightning to strike or the ten commandments of your personal career change to fall into your hands, you won't break free of a fixed mindset. Writing in *Harvard Business Review*, author and professor Herminia Ibarra said, "We change only when we have enticing alternatives that we can feel, touch, and taste. Working identity, as a practice, is necessarily a process of experimenting, testing, and learning about our possible selves. Insight in career change doesn't come first. We learn by doing."[27]

"While it's commonly thought that introspection leads to growth—we peer into ourselves and pull out our essence—in reality, action leads to change," Ibarra wrote. "We learn who we have become—in practice, not in theory—by testing fantasy and reality, not by 'looking inside.' Knowing oneself is crucial, but it is usually the outcome of—and not a first input to—the reinvention process. Worse, starting out by trying to identify one's true self often causes paralysis. While we wait for the flash of blinding insight, opportunities pass us by. To launch ourselves anew, we need to get out of our heads. We need to *act*."[28]

Psychologist Barry Kaufman explained in *The Week*, "Our most creative ideas don't tend to come when we're consciously focused on the problem. Great insights come through interacting with people, gaining experiences, and letting your mind make connections."[29]

THE IMPORTANCE OF ACTING

I know firsthand how important interactions are to reinvention. In fact, that's how the concept of this book was born. I had commented on a LinkedIn post by Eric Koester,

---

27 Herminia Ibarra, "How to Stay Stuck in the Wrong Career."
28 Ibid.
29 Eric Barker, "6 Science-Backed Tips for Boosting Your Creativity."

Georgetown University business school professor and founder of Creator Institute, and then forgot about it. About a month later, Koester messaged me on LinkedIn asking if I knew of any recent college graduates wanting to write a book. I had thought for years about writing a book on public relations but had never taken the leap. Certainly I was no recent college graduate. However, I responded to his note asking if he would consider a "mature" student. We spoke, and Koester agreed to my participation.

To my surprise, I was suddenly part of the book writing program Koester runs. At the start, I didn't even know what I would write about. Nor did I realize that this would change the arc of my career—that I had embarked on my own career reinvention. Sure, I had casually entertained ideas about my next act, but to be honest, I hadn't invested much time reflecting on it. However, once I was in action mode with the book project, things fell into place. My longtime interest in career reinvention and personal branding resurfaced. I had found what I wanted to do.

Psychologist and professor Cecilia Dintino wrote about the writer and cultural anthropologist Mary Catherine Bateson's view of life over fifty. Dintino said, "Bateson calls being over fifty 'Adulthood II' and says that since there is no script for this stage, we need to develop the skill of improvisation. Instead of resisting change and turbulence, grown-ups say, 'Yes, and.' In other words, we accept what comes and we make it into something worthwhile."[30]

---

30 Cecilia Dintino, "Growing Up Past 50."

Stasieczko has done this with his Innovation Channel, the series of videos he is creating on YouTube for the copying industry. "We're still developing it. It's a year old," he told me. "I didn't define this when I started it because I don't know where it's going to lead. But it's starting to lead more to this media venue."

Believing in a growth mindset implies being curious. "After all, if you don't believe it's possible to change, why would personal growth, learning, and curiosity be high on your priority list?" asked Dweck in her book, *Mindset*.[31]

Or as Gottberg said in The Senior List interview, "After all of the research I've uncovered, I am convinced that the most important trait any of us can have at any age is curiosity or inquisitiveness. Why? To me, curiosity implies that we remain open to new ideas and a willingness to continually keep learning. It also suggests that we are adaptable and open to change. Curiosity implies an optimistic, forward-thinking perspective rather than looking backward and wishing things were as they used to be instead of what is happening right now. The more we can nurture and encourage this character trait in ourselves and each other, the more resilient and the more optimistic we become."[32]

For Keller, a master at recreation, the essence of reinventing yourself later in life is to trust your gut, do something that interests you, and be courageous about trying something

---

31 Carol S. Dweck, "Growth Mindset: The Surprising Psychology of Self-Belief."

32 Amie Clark, "Expert Interview Series: Kathy Gottberg: Aging, and Living a Fulfilling Life."

new. "It won't always work. There's no magic formula," he said. "And that's why you need courage, because it might not work out."

Frederick G. Thompson, who had been a PR and marketing executive for thirty-five years, wasn't afraid to try something new. After he sold his PR and marketing agency at age fifty-five, he realized he was tired of PR but not ready to retire. PR had become more technology-driven, and he wasn't comfortable with that. He also knew that people weren't knocking down his door to hire a fifty-five-year-old.

"As I looked at my career, I discovered the thing that I enjoyed the most was working with organizations that made a difference." He was now at the point in his career where he wanted to give back.

Having worked with nonprofits at his agency, along with many for-profit companies, he had the skills to help nonprofits with marketing, positioning, brand building, management, and fundraising. He also knew his age would be viewed more favorably by nonprofits, where management skewed older. Using his marketing savvy, he reinvented himself as an executive for nonprofits, creating a compelling narrative. Just as he had helped companies like Citibank and IBM become profitable, he would do the same for nonprofits.

In less than a year, Thompson secured a position as president and CEO of the nonprofit the Jane Goodall Institute. He attributes his success to doing a skills assessment and understanding his strengths. Thompson provided a skills assessment inventory that I've included in the resource guide at the book's conclusion. "I wasn't going to become an auto mechanic or a TV repairman," he said. "I took the skills I had and recast them." His bet on himself paid off. Under his leadership, the organization grew fivefold.

"If you continue to do what you have always done, you will continue to know what you know today," wrote entrepreneur Scott Oldford. "No growth. No progress. No evolution. You need to surround yourself with new beliefs, concepts, and ideas that push your boundaries and force you to step out of your comfort zone. You need to question what you believe and know, and the only way to do this is to open your eyes (and ears)."[33]

Marci Alboher, author and vice president of Encore, a nonprofit that helps people pursue second acts, talked about a Zen concept of "beginner's mind" in an interview for Knowledge@Wharton. "You learn something new with the eyes of a beginner, and it's actually a pretty exciting thing," she said. "I think we all have the capacity to continue learning. If you become a lifelong learner, you will keep that skill from atrophying. It's a pretty important part of aging: to learn how to learn new things and to exercise that muscle often."[34]

---

33 Scott Oldford, "How to Upgrade Your Mindset and Defeat Your Biggest Obstacle as an Entrepreneur."

34 "Encore Careers: Why an Aging Population Is a Resource, Not a Problem."

THE FIVE STAGES OF CHANGE

In thinking about career reinvention, realize that a growth mindset, while essential, is not the whole story. Psychologists like to talk about the transtheoretical model of change, also known as the stages of change model. Traditionally, behavioral change was often seen as an event such as quitting smoking, drinking, or overeating, according to behavior change company Pro-Change. Instead, according to Pro-Change's website, "TTM recognizes change as a process that unfolds over time, involving progress through a series of stages. While this can occur in a linear fashion, a nonlinear progression is common. Often, individuals recycle through the stages or regress to earlier stages from later ones."[35]

The model posits that people typically go through five stages in changing behavior, beginning with being resistant to change, and at that stage, overemphasize the cons of doing so. In the next stage, they are able to think about change but may feel ambivalent about it. In the third stage, small steps are taken to begin to change behavior. In the fourth stage, people are able to take larger steps. And in the fifth stage, they work to maintain the change and not relapse.

The model also provides a framework for reinvention, implying that reinvention isn't a straight-line process, but one that involves zigs and zags. That means you shouldn't be hard on yourself if you take several steps backward

---

35 "Transtheoretical Model (Or Stages of Change)—Health Behavior Change."

before you move forward. Change takes time and should begin modestly. Alboher, in the Knowledge@Wharton interview, suggested laying your foundation for reinvention wisely by taking small steps. "Could you be exploring what interests you?" she asked. "Could you be taking some courses on the side? Could you be connecting with other people who are interested in this idea?"[36]

Clark advised planning ahead for a career reinvention. "Somebody in their forties should be doing this now," she told me. "Most people don't plan nearly as far in advance as they should. So many people think in six-month or twelve-month or even twenty-four-month increments. And really, if you want to have a thriving reinvention, start thinking now for the future in small ways. You can take small actions, and it pays a big dividend, about what you want to do in three years, or in five years."

On some level, you are hardwired to change. After all, civilization would not have evolved without that. Armed with a growth mindset, you have the moxie to improve. As Freedman reminded us, "The encore stage is not about 'clinging to our lost youth,'" he said. "Rather, it means harnessing our talents and knowledge in ways characterized by 'purpose, contribution, and commitment, particularly to the well-being of future generations.'"[37]

---

36 "Encore Careers: Why an Aging Population Is a Resource, Not a Problem."
37 Nancy Koehn, "The Aging of American, as Opportunity."

A FEW THINGS TO KEEP IN MIND

- Don't rest on your laurels. Adopt a beginner's mind.
- Don't paralyze yourself with thought. Act.
- Begin your reinvention by taking small steps.
- Don't expect reinvention to be a straight line. You'll zig and zag.

Now that we understand the importance of a growth mindset, let's look at the next principle of reinvention and rebranding: being uncomfortable.

YOUR TURN

Are you embracing a growth mindset? If not, what can you do differently to do so? What is holding you back? What baby steps can you take to try on a new guise? Write down a few activities you can easily do, then choose one and see how it feels. If it doesn't work, no problem. But recognize what you've learned about yourself before you take your next step.

CHAPTER 2

BEING UNCOMFORTABLE

———

"I haven't had a bolt of thunder and a flash of lightning appear signaling what I want to be. But for a long time in my life, I was waiting for that. Now I feel I can't wait. I need a job."

—GRACE M.

At age fifty-four, Grace M. (she requested that I not use her real name) was navigating that uncomfortable in-between space, out of work and under pressure to be hired but unwilling to settle. She was wistful she never had an epiphany revealing her life's path.

Sweaty palms, heavy breathing, the fear of people judging you poorly, the hesitancy to enter a room of strangers—you've had those moments where you'd rather hide than act. Yet to grow, learn, and change, you must travel in the land of discomfort. Avoiding that may control anxiety, but it will bind you, tying your wings.

A bit of a renegade, Grace often zigged when others zagged. She got a PhD in strategic management and organizational sociology because an MBA seemed too cookie-cutter. She managed a data warehouse and marketing analytics team when that was new and cutting-edge. And she created groundbreaking, data-driven, personalized marketing tactics for a large financial institution. For twenty-four years, she climbed the marketing hierarchy, getting bigger jobs with more responsibility. Most recently, she oversaw marketing for two start-ups headquartered in the UK and expanding into the United States where she was based.

Pouring her soul into these jobs, especially the last one, she exhausted her fervor. She ran into a buzz saw of cultural issues, unrealistic expectations, and unsupportive management. "It became very hard to run a global organization from the United States when there was no buy-in across the global leadership team," she said.

When a new CEO arrived in 2018 and brought in his own people, she lost her job. Burned out, she needed to get her bearings. Her one certainty was she didn't want another marketing job. She longed to hang her hat on something but couldn't picture it.

"I just want to say to a recruiter, 'Here's my skill set. Let me spread those cards on the table, and tell me what I'll be good at,'" she told me wishfully. "And you know, I'll take that direction."

Grace was running headlong into questions of identity and purpose. How does she talk about herself now that she has no job? "It's harder when I am around other people," she said. "When we are socializing, and I don't have a job to talk about, it's uncomfortable." She paused, adding sorrowfully, "I wouldn't say that I have stopped socializing or that I don't talk about my situation. But that's when it strikes me most. I'm still—to use that derogative term—without a new job."

THE STIGMA OF UNEMPLOYMENT

Losing a job pulls you adrift. In a flash, you've lost your routine, financial security, and connections. As Robert L. Leahy wrote in *Psychology Today* about unemployment, "Some people think, 'I am wearing a sign around my neck—unemployed, failure, unwanted.'"[38]

Unfortunately, the stigma of being unemployed is real. Researchers at UCLA found that people tended to "make negative associations about those who were unemployed, which often leads to unfair discrimination," according to columnist Lee Dye on ABC News' website. The unspoken assumption is "What is wrong with that person?"[39]

---

38   Robert H. Leahy, "Feeling Ashamed of Being Unemployed."
39   Lee Dye, "Unemployment: UCLA Study Shows Stigma of Joblessness Is Immediate."

To break the choke hold of unemployment, you must leave your comfort zone. "By being uncomfortable and trying different things, we can teach our brains new tricks and new ways of doing things," wrote Wanda Curlee, an associate professor at American Public University School of Business. "We can become more mentally flexible and, as a result, more creative and innovative."[40]

Trying different activities is one thing. Accepting our new image is another. Thinking of yourself in a new way takes time. Dorie Clark shared a story with me from her book, *Reinventing You*, about a woman who had been a teacher for many years before becoming an executive director of a nonprofit. When someone at a party asked her what she did, she replied, "I'm a teacher." The person then inquired what she taught. Caught flat-footed, she explained she wasn't teaching now. Afterward, her husband asked her why she didn't mention that she'd been running a nonprofit for three years. Until her husband's question, she hadn't realized her self-perception lagged reality.

UNDERSTAND YOURSELF

Not entirely comfortable with her situation, Grace couldn't help comparing herself unfavorably to others. Hesitating for a moment, her voice less steady, she said, "I look at other people in my network, people who are either close friends or

---

40 "Success Isn't Comfortable: Lessons in Leadership from the Human Capital Institute."

close associates my age or older, who are so accomplished in their careers," she said. "And I don't feel that way."

"Comparing ourselves with others is a game we can't win," bestselling author Daniel Pink concludes. Some people will always accomplish more than you, Pink said. "Accept that reality and don't let it destroy or undermine your efforts."[41]

Rather than look outward, your primary validation must be internal. "Before you can reinvent yourself, you need to know who you are," said Rebecca Webber in *Psychology Today*. Quoting Robert Steven Kaplan, president and CEO of the Federal Reserve Bank of Dallas and a former Harvard Business School dean and author of *What You're Really Meant to Do,* she wrote, "People need to understand their strengths, their weaknesses, their passions, and their own story. Then they can look at what's going on in the world and try to match themselves up to opportunities."[42]

"If you don't go through a process of self-discovery but just accept others' decisions, ten years later, you might find yourself saying, 'I don't think that's me,'" John Mayer, a professor of psychology at the University of New Hampshire and the author of *Personal Intelligence* said in Webber's *Psychology Today* article.[43]

41 Tami Kamin Meyer, "You Can Reinvent Yourself, No Matter Your Age."

42 Rebecca Webber, "Reinvent Yourself."

43 Ibid.

Looking inward is easier said than done. Knowing yourself and where you will fit in is hard but glossing over imperfections or diminishing accomplishments is easy. That's why support groups that connect you to others with similar experience can be powerful.

GETTING COMFORTABLE WITH BEING UNCOMFORTABLE

In an article in *Strategy+Business*, Sally Helgesen, an author and leadership development coach, related a story of Brigadier General Marianne Watson. Having retired in her early fifties from her position as director of manpower and personnel for the US Army and Air National Guard and recently lost her husband, Watson felt adrift. She had no support network because few women were at her level in the military.

"I didn't see a path forward, and I had no idea of what kind of opportunities were out there or what I could do," she told Helgesen.[44]

That changed when Watson joined a transition program for senior women called Mission: Getting to Next. The program helped her see "that it was OK to be confused and vulnerable when I was in the process of trying to figure things out."[45]

---

44 Sally Helgesen, "Helping Women Leaders Plot Their Next Career Move."

45 Ibid.

Roy T. Bennett, author of *The Light in the Heart*, said, "You never change your life until you step out of your comfort zone."[46]

Grace, as she tried to move on, was caught between believing she'd missed the success train and knowing it didn't matter. "I am who I am," she said proudly. "I have lots of other interests besides my job. My days are full." Even though she was not working, she discovered fabulous things about not working. Her voice dropping, she added, "But I don't feel like I'm allowed to pretend that I'm retired. Because I'm not. I'm looking for a job."

Grace is part of the largest class of people her age working or looking for work. The majority of baby boomers (US adults born 1946 to 1964) are still working. The oldest of them are in the labor force at record rates, according to Pew Research Center. Age sixty-five is no longer the magic retirement number, and twenty-nine percent of boomers age sixty-five to seventy-two are working or seeking work.[47] Boomers are also defying the stereotype that starting a business is for younger people. Those age fifty-five to sixty-four represented more than a quarter of new entrepreneurs in 2018, an unprecedented number due to the aging of the population, according to the 2018 Kauffman National Report on Early-Stage Entrepreneurship.[48]

---

46 Roy T. Bennett, "Change Begins at the End of Your Comfort Zone."
47 Richard Fry, "Baby Boomers Are Staying in the Labor Force at Rates Not Seen in Generations for People Their Age."
48 Julie Scheidegger, "Indicators Provide Early-Stage Entrepreneurship Data."

To reinvent yourself, or at least begin to change your spots, you need to embrace the paradox of being comfortable with being uncomfortable to take risks. Otherwise, you retreat into the security of doing only what you know. In fact, research shows that growth doesn't happen without some discomfort.

Scientists demonstrated this with an experiment with monkeys. As freelance writer Jessica Stillman related in *Inc.*, monkeys were rewarded if they hit a particular target. Sometimes they were rewarded often, other times less frequently. If the monkeys predicted which target would pay off, their brain regions associated with learning shut down. When they couldn't guess, their learning areas lit up.[49] Not knowing what comes next is the optimal way to grow.

> To reinvent yourself, or at least begin to change your spots, you need to embrace the paradox of being comfortable enough with being uncomfortable to take risks. Otherwise, you retreat into the security of doing only what you know.

---

49 Jessica Stillman, "Science Has Just Confirmed That If You're Not Outside Your Comfort Zone, You're Not Learning."

THRIVING ON CHANGE

Chip Conley's learning areas glowed when he joined Airbnb at age fifty-two after its founders recruited him. A fish out of water, Conley was twice the age of the average Airbnb employee. For twenty-four years, he had owned and run over fifty boutique hotels under his Joie de Vivre (joy of living) brand, making him the second largest boutique hotelier in the United States. He had no social media bona fides, was clueless about the sharing economy, and tech lingo was a foreign language to him.

A lesser person might have fled to the nearest exit. However, Conley was born with a curiosity gene. Rather than bolt, he accepted feeling uncomfortable. He listened and learned, discovering that his "wise eyes" could benefit from their "fresh eyes."[50]

"Most fascinating to me was how much (the young Airbnb employees) had to offer me, as much as I had to offer them," he said in an interview.[51]

BEING UNCOMFORTABLE IS ESSENTIAL FOR GROWTH

Assuming a mantle of company elder, Conley recruited one hundred Airbnb mentees to share experiences and insights. "That's the new sharing economy—sharing wisdom across generations."

---

50 Melissa Locker, "Airbnb's Chip Conley Is Doubling Down on Being a 'Modern Elder.'"

51 "Chip Conley, Modern Elder Academy."

His cross-generation work helped Airbnb earn one of the highest customer satisfaction ratings across the hospitality industry and set the stage for Conley's next act, the founding of the Modern Elder Academy, the world's first midlife wisdom school. There, middle-aged workers get the chance to "reset, restore, and repurpose" their lives through one- or two-week programs in Baja California, Mexico.

Author and coach Brad Stulberg, shared the story of big-wave surfer Nic Lamb who discovered that being uncomfortable is a prerequisite to riding four-story waves. "He learned that while you can pull back, you can almost always push through," Stulberg wrote. For Lamb, Stulberg said, "'Pushing through is courage. Pulling back is regret.'"[52]

Overall, Grace was riding the waves of discomfort well. "On the whole, I feel optimistic," she said. "I feel like something is going to work out. I don't know what that is. And it's hard. If I could just open the curtain and push away the fog, it's there. I can see it. I'm a very avid outdoors person. And I love maps. And maps help get you to where you want to go. And if you're lost, you look at the map, and you can get there." Quietly, she said, "There is no map for me right now."

Traveling without a navigation guide isn't comfortable, but sometimes you just need to do it. As James Altucher wrote, "Don't look to find the end of the road when you are still at

---

52   Brad Stulberg, "A Simple Equation Can Teach Us to Get Better Every Day."

the very first step. Dorothy couldn't see Oz when she first walked on the yellow brick road."[53]

MOVING AHEAD

For Grace, the discovery process was ongoing. "I'm continuing to do self-reflection, to see if something else would make sense for me to pursue." She meditated, read, talked to friends, and journaled, all of which kept her grounded.

To help the fog recede, Grace checked in regularly with a network of supportive friends. She also served on the advisory board and created educational materials for an organization called amazing community, a nonprofit that helps women over fifty thrive.

Widening her vista, she planned to attend professional conferences. "I will meet someone who is going to see the twinkle in my eye and we're going to connect, and they will have a position that they're trying to fill," she said assuredly.

Grace acknowledged she was doing OK, except for times when an inner voice interrupted her progress, which she called the "I should have this figured out by now" message.

"And when I don't go there, then I'm OK," she continued. "Because who's to say that my story needs to be any particular way. Right? You know it's up and down. And fortunately, for me, it's mostly up." Her voice breaking, she said that

---

53   James Altucher, "The Ultimate Guide to Reinventing Yourself."

sometimes she's "applied for another job and maybe had it go one round. It's not much fun. And other times, I can be OK and be happy to have the flexibility to take care of my physical and mental health, ride my bike, and walk outside if it's a beautiful, gorgeous day. My personal life would be much harder to do if I were working sixty or seventy hours a week."

A FEW THINGS TO KEEP IN MIND

- Get comfortable with being uncomfortable. You will push through the discomfort.
- Stepping out of your comfort zone is necessary for change.
- Support groups can help you do the necessary self-discovery so in ten years you're not wondering what happened.

How do we move beyond being uncomfortable? Let's discover the next principle of reinvention and rebranding: willingness to learn.

YOUR TURN

What makes you uncomfortable about reinventing yourself? What have you been avoiding doing because it makes you squirm? Ask yourself, what is the worst thing that can happen if you do this? What is the best outcome? How can you mitigate the downside and plow on? Sometimes taking baby steps is a safer, surer, more comfortable way to move toward your goal.

CHAPTER 3

WILLINGNESS TO LEARN

"I celebrate my failures. I mitigate my risk so I can experiment often and fail safely. This is a big factor in fast reinvention."

–LEWIS SCHIFF, AUTHOR AND *INC.* COLUMNIST

At age forty, Keith Keller's career trajectory was nose-diving. His moon shot to be a rock musician in Melbourne, Australia, couldn't pay the bills. He didn't just hate his day job working at a call center, he *despised* it. To succeed at the call center, he had to transcribe a previous call while answering another call. Keller, for the life of him, couldn't do two things at once.

"I remember going to a café every day and locking myself in the courtyard. I would pull apart all the strategies of how

I was able to do correspondence while I was talking," Keller recalled. "And it didn't matter what I tried. I couldn't do it."

Keller didn't know it then, but he would turn his inability to do two things at once into a life hack that transformed his life.

Realizing he would never crack the call center code, he visited a career counselor who recommended that he, too, become a career counselor. He liked the idea of helping other people avoid the crummy jobs he had endured. At age forty, he quit his call center job and returned to school to obtain a certificate in career counseling. As someone who absorbed more by doing than by reading, he obtained a part-time job where he was paid to learn on the job for three days while he studied on the other two days.

A year later, he had his career counselor certificate but no job. A friend suggested that they start a radio show. He had always wanted to be a radio announcer, but other people thought he was nuts. "Everyone in my world told me, 'It won't work,'" Keller said.

Keller ignored the warnings, and in 2008, he and his friend created Career Success Radio for Blog Talk Radio. Keller tapped into his experience with bad jobs and his knowledge of career counseling to motivate others. Geared toward people who hated to go to work, the show featured people who successfully changed jobs, went back to school, or otherwise reinvented their work life. People from 127 countries tuned in, and over two years, Career Success Radio got eighty thousand downloads. Still, Keller endured another hurdle. The radio show succeeded in attracting an audience, but it failed on the financial side. It didn't attract sponsors.

Keller's experience illustrated that the path of reinvention is often crooked with zigs and zags. As Bradley R. Staats noted in his book *Never Stop Learning: Stay Relevant, Reinvent Yourself, and Thrive*, reinvention involves learning, failing, and growing.

"We can't just be knowledge workers," Staats wrote. "We must also be learning workers. You can't expect to learn and grow without taking some missteps."[54]

Keller's life exemplifies that. "Not everything works," he said. "So I've learned to practice this phrase—fail fast. I hung onto that radio show for two years. If I were very clever, I would have let it go earlier. I looked back on that and said, 'I'm never hanging on to stuff for two years.' I'll go really hard for six to twelve months, but if the writing's on the wall, I will move on."

Similar to Keller, Kevin Daum, author and entrepreneur, embraced what he called "failing loudly." "It's hard after a massive failure like mine (he lost his mortgage company in the 2008 recession) to get over the embarrassment and talk about it," he wrote in *Inc.* "But I did. In fact, I shared my failures with my friends and advisors so often even I got tired of hearing about them. But all that sharing helped me to analyze and learn from those failures and learn a new and

---

54   Bradley R. Staats, "Don't Just Dive Into Action: Stop to Think First."

better path. Now I celebrate my failures. I mitigate my risk so I can experiment often and fail safely. This is a big factor in fast reinvention."[55]

The path of reinvention is often crooked with zigs and zags.

NEVER STOP LEARNING

Keller didn't switch gears only when something didn't work. Like a professional athlete constantly perfecting his skill, he was forever tweaking and transforming himself. He knew that nothing stayed the same, and he needed to change to stay on top of his game.

Writer Rebecca Webber explained that reinvention required change. Quoting Kaplan again, the former Harvard Business School dean, she wrote, "The world is not stagnant, and you are not stagnant. The dreams you have today may no longer be your goals two, three, or five years from now. Even if they are, the progress you're making toward them today may not satisfy you in the future."[56]

Mitchell Levy knew about changing lanes frequently. Over the course of his thirty-five-year-career, he has been a financial systems analyst, ecommerce consultant, CMO, CEO, futurist, executive coach, board member of a NASDAQ-listed company,

---

55   Kevin Daum, "5 Tips for Successful Reinvention."
56   Rebecca Webber, "Reinvent Yourself."

and CEO of a "done-for-you" publishing firm where he was its first ghostwriter. Like Keller, Levy had an aptitude for seizing opportunities. You wouldn't have guessed that, though, knowing Levy as a boy.

Growing up in three different towns in New Jersey, Levy was the type of kid you wanted to shake. A late bloomer, he sleepwalked through his classes, didn't study, and focused on having fun. "It wasn't because of trauma or any issues," he told me. "I wasn't prepared to start life."

At age eighteen, he enrolled at the University of Miami, which was known as a party school. In his first semester, he met two gorgeous girls. Little did he know at the time that hanging out with these two women would change his life. Or that his ability to seize an opportunity would become a catalyst for his career.

The women were not only beautiful but also studious. Rather than going to the beach, they hit the books in the library. Levy, eager to get to know them, trailed along and started studying and applying himself.

"I was finally doing something for me," he told me. "It was my decision rather than my mom saying, 'You have to go to school.'"

Now focused, he found the courses too easy. Rather than coast through school, he asked his counselor about the most difficult major in the business school. He was told about Stochastic and Deterministic Models of Operations Research, a mouthful of a name. Undeterred, Levy switched his major, opening up the world of optimization. A business concept, operations research provides a framework for analyzing and improving systems. At school, Levy learned how a penny reduction in meat costs at Burger King saved the company millions of dollars. The impact of that lesson was never forgotten.

Levy didn't realize that the concept of operations research would become a through line in his life. Recalling his career, he told me, "Operations research taught me the frameworks of how to move to the next direction and what I needed to do to get there. Most of the world has a hard time deciding which way to go if they come to a fork in a road. I find it easy to identify what decision to make."

Levy applied that same determination in his personal life. When he was twenty-six, he spotted a beautiful, blonde woman with a halo around her at a bus stop. He offered her a ride to work, and she turned him down. He ran into her the next day and discovered where she worked. He asked her out more than twenty times until she finally said yes. They have now been married thirty years.

After getting his MBA, Levy worked in systems and finance for a succession of small and large companies. Using his knowledge of frameworks, Levy developed a formula for success. "I realized that although I only spoke the English language, I was able to speak marketing, sales, investments, and boardroom. I can put myself in the mindset of the other person and have a completely different framework of thinking based on the person I'm talking with."

THE FRAMEWORK MODEL

When he was thirty-four, Levy was ready for a change. Rather than simply applying for jobs, he used a framework a mentor had shared with him called the river model.

"So imagine you're on one side of the river, and you want to get to the other," Levy explained. "The other side of the river is where you want to get with your career. First, you have to define who you want to be tomorrow. And then you define the characteristics of who you are today. As you're crossing the river, you see rocks. Some of the rocks go forward, some go sideways, some go backward, some are slippery. The question is—when crossing the river or when crossing life—which rocks you take, and sometimes you have to go backward to go forward."

Applying the river model to his own life opened Levy's eyes to what he needed to do. Recognizing that his name wasn't known outside Sun Microsystems, where he was running the ecommerce part of Sun's operations division, he spent the next three years building his personal brand. He volunteered to be the Sun representative for a nonprofit ecommerce organization, allowing him to be quoted in the media. He booked a young Jeff Bezos to speak at the organization's trade show and participated on a panel with Mark Cuban.

When he left his corporate job, Levy's first client was a former boss at Sun Microsystems. The client wanted him to do SEO, or search engine optimization, optimizing content for discovery in search engines. Levy was not an expert on SEO and thought it beneath a top consultant. But putting on his framework optimization hat, he decided to make it work. In two weeks, he purchased every training program on the market and became an SEO expert, reading everything on the subject. He carved out a deal with his client where he was paid $10,000 for each SEO client sold. In a short time, they sold five. Learning a new skill had paid off.

THE ART OF FAILING

Keller, too, continued to change directions. Despite the failure of his radio show, Keller created another business from its ashes in the early days of social media. Keller posted links to the show on Facebook, LinkedIn, and Twitter. Only Twitter generated traffic.

People took notice of Keller's social media posts and asked, "How do you do this Twitter thing?" That led to Keller's next reinvention as a Twitter colossus.

"I decided I am going to be the Twitter dude," he said. "I'm going to be world famous as the Twitter guy. I never use Snapchat. I don't use Instagram. I hardly ever use Facebook or YouTube. I started a Pinterest account, but I never use it."

By focusing exclusively on Twitter, Keller turned his inability to focus on two things at once into an asset. "That's my hack for life," he told me. Today, Keller has over 58 million followers on Twitter and is ranked among the top B2B digital influencers in the world by thought leadership platform Digital360.

Beyond his dead-on focus, Keller's Twitter success was a tribute to his humility and a subtle indictment of how Twitter influencers often work. Calling what he does Twitter Magic 123, Keller developed a three-pronged approach that began with following people first. Most Twitter influencers are extremely selective in following people and have many more followers than people they follow. Not Keller.

"People ask, 'What are you following people for? You're famous,'" he told me. "No. I'm not that famous," he said. "Lots of people haven't heard of me. And I'm humble enough to follow them first and start a conversation. And after that, I have had some amazing conversations. I'm so proud of my mindset."

Keller went out of his way to help people on Twitter. In fact, I met Keller on Twitter when, to my surprise, he actively promoted a blog post of mine, created a graphic to enhance it, and garnered attention for it. I decided he was someone I wanted to know.

A true Twitter evangelist, Keller shared his Twitter craft through individual coaching sessions. While coaching, Keller began another reinvention using his talent to spot opportunity where most people see problems. His latest reinvention was rethinking conferences, combining a virtual and real model to magnify the impact of a conference.

For Keller, the essence of reinventing yourself later in life is to trust your gut, do something that interests you, and be brave about trying something new.

TO THINE OWN SELF BE TRUE

While courage is essential to reinvention, it's not the only key. Equally important is the ability to be self-aware. Author and reinvention career coach John Tarnoff told me, "Reinvention is really about the willingness to be open, to drill down and follow the authentic calling that we can discover at this time in our life. We now have the knowledge to make the kinds of changes and course corrections to set our paths on a more productive, more enjoyable, more resonant, and more meaningful career path."

In *Psychology Today*, Robert Steven Kaplan said, "People need to understand their strengths, their weaknesses, their passions, and their own story. Then they can look at what's going on in the world and try to match themselves up to opportunities."[57]

Keller knew how to choose the right path. At age fifty-four, he cherished the idea that he was doing what he wanted. He said to ask yourself, "'Do I want all the shiny things and the job I hate? Or do I want to be happy and live on less?' If

---

57   Rebecca Webber, "Reinvent Yourself."

you can drop the need for all the latest gadgets and all the expenses, it frees you up to explore and trust and do a few of those scary things that maybe only you can do."

Along the way, Keller learned that to do his best work, he needed to allot two or three hours a day without distractions. "You can't spend only an hour a month or you might as well not do it at all," he told me. "The big chunks of time allow me to get set for the miracles to happen."

Keller, through ups and downs, learned what he did best. He loved to try new things, especially technology, to touch items and pull them apart. "I'm the guy who goes first and tries it, and then I back up and say, 'OK, I've done it. Just follow me. I know the way. I've done the walk before.' And I love that positioning. That's my role in the world."

While courage is essential to reinvention, it's not the only key. Equally important is the ability to be self-aware.

Levy, too, played to his strengths, seizing opportunities and turning them into pure gold. He transformed a small teaching gig at San José State University into an ecommerce certificate program where he got twenty-five percent of the revenues but no salary. The school thought it was a good deal until they sold over 4,400 courses, grossing over $2 million and reluctantly wrote Levy checks for his share.

Between his consulting, speaking, and teaching, Levy became known as Mr. Ecommerce. But then the dot-com bust occurred in 2002, and Levy's speaking and consulting tanked. To put that period in context, by the end of the stock market downturn of 2002, stocks had lost $5 trillion in market capitalization since the peak. Once robust companies like CDNow and eToys.com were among many ecommerce companies that folded or lost much of their value. To stay afloat, Levy ran a CEO networking group and segued his consulting work into thought leadership, helping executives, coaches, and other individuals become better known.

Using his framework of optimizing business, he pivoted into book publishing, recognizing it as the ultimate badge of thought leadership. A book would give his clients instant recognition.

"I looked at the publishing industry," Levy said, "and I realized a major transformation was going to happen, where everyone had a camera, a microphone, and a platform available to them to create their own shows and books, their own thought leadership. I was able to merge the thought leadership work I was doing with the work I was doing with publishing."

In 2005, at age forty-five, he reinvented himself as a publisher. Between 2005 and 2017, he published eight hundred books, including a number of Amazon bestsellers. Unlike a typical traditional publisher, whose books take a year or more to get published, his books crossed the finish line in two to four months. He made most of his money through book sales.

His business, like most, had good years and bad. In plum years, he rented a house in Europe for family and friends for four weeks; in hard times, he laid off some contract workers and stayed in the United States. The sticking point was that the publishing business wasn't a guaranteed sales bull's-eye. In addition, because so many books were being published, it became tougher to get noticed.

At the end of 2016, he ran a Kickstarter campaign to raise money to build an automation tool for sharing book content on Twitter. Those ponying up the most money were guaranteed publication of a book. Twenty people qualified. A year later, only three of the twenty people had written a book that under Levy's system would take only eight hours to write.

"So seventeen people couldn't find eight hours in a twelve-month period," he said, "to do something that would be worthwhile to them and that they paid for."

That was an aha moment for Levy. Shortly afterward, he gave a TED Talk on thought leadership that helped him see he was focused on the wrong audience. "It made me think about my business from a different perspective. I realized the people I wanted to serve weren't those who wanted to write a book but those who didn't have time to write their own book." Like Keller, he wasn't afraid to admit he needed to change.

At age fifty-seven, Levy pivoted again by embracing a new framework. Instead of thinking of himself as a publisher for people who wanted to write books, he positioned himself as someone "who makes successful people more successful." His new business included ghostwriting books for executives, coaches, speakers, and large and small corporations. His services helped authors promote their books and drive more business.

This latest pivot required new skills. He enrolled in a two-day branding program to create a consistent look and feel for his business on social media and his website. He spent all of 2018 redefining his internal processes to make it easy for people to do business with him, including hiring new people, partnering with others, and changing his messaging and positioning. To ensure his writers were able to ghostwrite books, he developed his own writing school.

Once Levy had his messaging in place, he invested in emails, newsletters, and social media to get the word out. He learned that his best approach was to have people book a strategy session with him where he often got them to take the next step. He used his over twenty thousand followers on LinkedIn to help promote his new business. And he found that paid ads on LinkedIn also performed well.

Looking back, Levy, now age fifty-nine, said that he is passing his framework model on to his clients. "I think that if I look at the end result of who I am now, it's helping other people establish frameworks to be more successful for themselves." Despite all his reinventions, Levy had returned to his core skill of building frameworks.

"If you're over fifty, you have such a tremendous wealth of skills and ability to give back to the world," said Levy. "I've always looked for an opportunity where I can give back to an audience and have fun helping people be successful. I'm at a really good stage of life, because I'm more focused than I've ever been with a product people need and still want. So yeah, I'm at a very happy place."

A FEW THINGS TO KEEP IN MIND

- Reinvention involves learning, failing, and growing.
- Practice failing fast.
- Rebranding and reinvention are lifelong processes. You're always tweaking.
- Courage and self-awareness will anchor your reinvention.

Now that you know that it's OK to fail as you try out new careers, let's consider the next principle of reinvention and rebranding: finding your purpose.

YOUR TURN

How have you reinvented or changed careers in the past? What can you learn from that in doing another reinvention? What have you wanted to try but were scared to do? List a few goals. Map out some baby steps you can take to test the waters before you go all in.

CHAPTER 4

FINDING YOUR PURPOSE

———

"The process of reinvention starts with reframing. You may look in the mirror and think you've always been a kitty cat. But you can look in that mirror and realize you're a lion."

—JOHN TARNOFF, AUTHOR AND REINVENTION COACH

At age fifty, Patrice Tanaka was burned out. Between caring for her sick husband and running a PR and marketing agency, she was working sixty to seventy hours a week.

"I was so depressed, I could barely get out of bed in the morning," Tanaka told me.

She was supporting her husband, who had been battling a brain tumor for sixteen years, while trying to build her agency and satisfy clients and professional and civic organizations.

"I just ran out of gas," she said.

At the end of her rope, she sought an executive coach. To her annoyance, the coach immediately told her to rethink her life's mission. "I can barely get out of bed and the first thing she asked me to do was to rethink my purpose in life," she recalled. Nevertheless, she thought about her coach's advice and something came to mind.

Two weeks later, returning to her coach, she revealed how haunted she was by the nearly three thousand people who had died five months earlier on September 11, 2001. She could see the twin towers from her lower Manhattan office and couldn't erase the image of people leaving for work but not returning home. It opened her eyes to life's sudden turns. She aspired to be "good to go," any time, having lived fully. "I told my coach that my purpose in life was to choose joy every day, to be mindful of that joy, and to share that joy with others," she said.

Her coach asked what brought her joy. Tanaka laughed, since nothing did so. Her coach persisted—maybe one thing had given her pleasure. To her surprise, Tanaka blurted out, "I love to dance." At age eight, growing up on the films of Fred Astaire and Ginger Rogers, her dream was to dance like Ginger Rogers. She imagined living in Manhattan, wearing long, flowing evening gowns and dancing in swank supper clubs wrapped in the arms of Fred Astaire. When she moved to Manhattan in her early twenties, her Ginger Rogers dream was forgotten, until that coaching session thirty years later.

Her homework was to book a dance lesson. A half hour before her next coaching session, she scheduled her first one. At age fifty, she found a new passion, and with weekly lessons, eventually won some championships. At her first session with her coach, she hadn't realized it, but rediscovering what she loved would change her life.

YOUR LIFE PURPOSE

What is your life purpose?

As a child of the sixties, I'm a sucker for self-help slogans like "be all you can be" and "live your best self." Although well meaning, the mantras dumb down the hard work of finding your purpose. Your life mission doesn't spring to life fully formed. You need to discover—or recover—it.

To find your purpose, you must claim your own life, which often gets lost in the day-to-day shuffle. "A lot of people fear that if they discover their life purpose, they're going to have to quit their day job," said Tanaka. "And then how will they pay the rent? And I tell them, 'Your life purpose isn't about your job or your career. It's about your life. It's accomplishing what matters most using your talents, expertise, and passion to serve others and the planet.'"

As the poet Mary Oliver asked, "What is it you plan to do with your one wild and precious life?"[58]

Determining your life purpose often takes a back seat until a life event opens your eyes. "It could be divorce, a death of a spouse, or the kids leaving home," Tanaka said. "All of a sudden, your life changes. You look around and you have more time. You realize the life that you've built or distracted yourself with isn't as fulfilling and satisfying as you thought it would be. Because for decades, we can avoid, ignore, or just be oblivious to our own needs." Then life intervenes.

For John Tarnoff, a career reinvention coach and the author of *Boomer Reinvention*, the trigger was a failing business and an accident. In 2001, the economic bubble had burst. His tech start-up was bleeding people and his relationship with his business partner was going south. "It was a terrible time of contraction," he recalled.

One Friday afternoon, he was skimming leaves from his pool when he lost his footing and fell into the pool. On the way down, he cracked his right shin on the side of the pool and broke his tibia. The crack literally changed his life. The accident helped him take stock of his goals. Seeking more self-awareness, at age fifty, he enrolled in a master's program in spiritual psychology at a small local college.

A month into the program, a fellow student shared that he had received a fantastic job offer with exceptional benefits. "And

---

58   Mary Oliver, *House of Light.*

it was miraculous," Tarnoff recalled. "Whatever he asked for, he got. And I'm sitting there thinking, 'Oh, great. Miracles are for other people, not for me.'" He stopped himself. Why couldn't he also live out his dreams? "Through the course of the program, I realized that it's possible for all of us to create our own miracles," he said. That realization changed his trajectory.

During his thirty-five-year career, Tarnoff had run through eighteen jobs and was fired from seven of them. He had gone through setbacks and recoveries with a lot of dodging and weaving to stay afloat. Frustrated, he viewed his experiences as recovering from disappointments. However, not everyone considered his career a failure.

He ran into an acquaintance at a networking event who lavishly praised how he handled his career. Tarnoff was shocked that his career misadventures were deemed successful. But after the colleague shared his admiration for Tarnoff's presence at the forefront of industries, Tarnoff viewed his career with fresh eyes. Sure, he had taken his eye off the ball and hadn't performed as well as expected. But he realized that had been his choice.

"I have a quest to find out new things," he said. "I sort of fired myself from these jobs because I got itchy." Rather than view his firings as shameful, he reframed them. "I was ready to leave."

His self-perception crystallized in 2012 when he gave a TEDx talk on transformation. Tarnoff got a chance to reexamine his life and recast it as an act of reinvention. "The process starts with reframing," he said in his talk. "You may look in the mirror and think you've always been a kitty cat. But you can look in that mirror and realize you're a lion."

It was Tarnoff's time to roar. He had found his purpose as a reinvention coach, helping people of all ages find their ideal career through personal growth.

> To find your purpose, you must claim your own life, which often gets lost in the day-to-day shuffle.

HAPPINESS AND REFRAMING

Living with purpose is a prescription for health and well-being. According to psychologist Larissa Rainey, "A strong sense of purpose in life has been found to build a wide variety of positive psychological outcomes."[59] Health and fitness author Bob Condor wrote that studies show that individuals who feel a "meaningfulness" or purpose in life report less pain and reduced anxiety over a six-month period than volunteer subjects who score lower for meaning in their lives.[60]

Finding your purpose is not a relentless search for meaning or a chance to have a pom-pom-filled rah-rah about the joys

---

59 Larisa Rainey, "The Search for Purpose in Life: An exploration of Purpose, the Search Process and Purpose Anxiety."
60 Bob Condor, "Purpose in Life = Happiness."

of life. Rather, it's a progression of "clearing out the clutter and silencing the noise so your true core is more tangible for the world and for yourself. This shift will allow you to find purpose and experience meaning along the journey, not just when the destination is reached," said Jesse Sostrin, director at PwC's US Leadership Coaching Center of Excellence.[61] Just as you may need a life crisis to find your purpose, so too a life crisis can upend your sense of identity.

That's what happened to Rita G. At age sixty-nine, Rita lost a job she had held and enjoyed for thirty years. "All of a sudden, you lose your sense of self. I wasn't who I was before," she said, her voice filled with emotion. "Sixty to seventy percent of that is gone."

As director of a university counseling and advising center, her identity was tied to being a professional in higher education, helping students, and interacting with other education professionals and faculty. "I was with smart, interesting people," she said. "People used to say to me, 'You're one of the few people I know who really likes her job.' I did really like my job, so giving that up was hard."

What do you do when your day-to-day life vanishes? For Rita, her routine had disappeared. "I'm goal-directed. I like to have structure," she said. "So all this free floating is tough. Getting up at a different time every day, having each day different. I look at my calendar a thousand times during the week. I don't love that. It makes me anxious."

---

61 Jesse Sostrin, "What to Do When Success Leaves You Empty."

She didn't have the luxury of lolling around. For financial reasons, she needed to work at least part-time. Trying to find a job, she'd been smacked down by ageism. Putting herself out on the job market was especially hard "as a quote, unquote old person," she admitted. "It made me more aware of how old I am. We baby boomers don't think of ourselves as old. But then you go and talk to people, and it's usually indirect, but they will say they aren't looking for someone with my experience. And if you look around at the other staff, everybody is younger," she said dejectedly. "I feel like a misfit."

To move on and find her purpose, Rita had to understand and view her experience differently. It meant changing her attitude and strengthening her coping skills, which took time. She found it "hard to get the motivation to look for something else until" she processed what was happening to her. Processing for Rita was analogous to going through the five stages of grief. Over the last two and a half years since she lost her job, she has experienced denial, anger, bargaining, depression, and now acceptance.

Along the way, she learned to discard expectations of finding another job or living a structured life. In other words, she altered her purpose and her sense of self. They were no longer tied to what she was and her old job, but to who she was now.

"I'm more used to my life now than before. I feel like I'm moving in the direction of getting my purpose back," Rita said, her voice strong. At this life stage, she knew her purpose wouldn't feel the same. "You know it's different, so your expectations and your sense of purpose have to be different," she said. "You have to change your expectations of who you are and what defines you and see how that works out rather than recreating the past." Rita's gradual self-acceptance helped her redefine her purpose.

PUTTING PURPOSE INTO ACTION

For Tanaka, finding and living her purpose changed her life, bringing her joy that fueled new opportunities. She winnowed out some activities to accommodate her husband and her professional obligations and allow time for her ballroom dancing. Since she stated, "I love to dance," that fateful day in her coach's office, she wrote two books, helped several nonprofits, and started her consultancy, Joyful Planet, which "helps individuals and organizations discover and live their life purpose."

"I've accomplished more in the past eighteen years than I had in the previous thirty-six," she said. "This is why I believe discovering and living our purpose is a powerful, 'competitive advantage'"—it focuses and drives you to accomplish what's most important.

Finding your purpose doesn't come prepackaged in a fortune cookie or from gazing outward. People often err, Tanaka said, by turning the concept of finding a purpose into a paint-by-numbers exercise. Instead of understanding themselves, they research, identify, and pursue lucrative careers. "They are going to be better served looking inside themselves," she said. "Only after you decide what you really love doing and do well should you look at that list of the most lucrative jobs and see if something fits with your own strengths and interests."

Don't be in a rush to find your purpose. The Franciscan priest and author Richard Rohr, in his book *Falling Upward*, talked about our staggering to find ourselves in the second part of our lives. We have "a sense of necessary suffering, of stumbling over stumbling stones and lots of shadowboxing, but often just a desire for ourselves, for something more, or what I call homesickness," Rohr wrote. "The first half of life is discovering the script, and the second half is actually writing it and owning it."[62]

Finding your purpose doesn't come prepackaged in a fortune cookie or from gazing outward.

Rita was in the process of writing her script. "I'm adjusting. I'm working part-time, I'm taking a class and volunteering," she said, sounding surprised by how far she had come. "I'm redefining what my roles are and how that can also make me feel more purposeful."

Rita's day-to-day life was a far cry from her previous structured days. But she had grown more comfortable.

---

62   Richard Rohr, Falling Upward. (55)

"I don't have to get up at a certain time," she said. "Today I woke up at nine thirty. I still haven't put on my makeup, and it's now twelve o'clock. And it's doable. I'm walking around the house and I'm dressed, but I'm wearing clothes I wouldn't wear outside. I have to go do a few things. But it's OK if I do it at two o'clock in the afternoon instead of at nine o'clock in the morning. So it's just more fluid."

Over the past year, Rita's sense of self had grown. Recently, she reviewed the schedule for some adult classes and surprised herself with her selection. While her old self would have chosen history, literature, or world news, she enrolled in a watercolor class. "I'm letting go of the intellectual side and turning to the more creative to see if that will be a pathway for me to explore more. It's a little bit looser and more imaginative."

Tanaka, since finding her purpose, was far along on her journey. Her emotional shape-shifting had brought her contentment. "I love PR but helping people with their purpose brings me great joy," she said. "So yes, I am absolutely happier. And the more I do it, the more joy and opportunities it brings me. So for me, choosing joy begets more joy." Finding your purpose, while not always easy, will be transformative, giving you the fuel to power your reinvention.

A FEW THINGS TO KEEP IN MIND
- Living with purpose is a prescription for health and well-being.

- Reinventing yourself involves altering your sense of purpose and sense of self.
- Your life purpose isn't handed to you. You may have to stumble first before you find it. And it may take time.

Now that you know the importance of finding your purpose, let's consider the next principle of reinvention and rebranding: storytelling.

YOUR TURN

Nick Craig and Scott A. Snook in *Harvard Business Review* suggest asking yourself these three questions to find your purpose and to do so in a small group of peers.[63] Here are their questions:

- What did you especially love doing when you were a child, before the world told you what you should or shouldn't like or do? Describe a moment and how it made you feel.
- What are two of your most challenging life experiences? How have they shaped you?
- What do you enjoy doing in your life now that helps you sing your song?

After you do that, create a clear, memorable statement of purpose:

My purpose is _____.

---

63   Nick Craig and Scott A. Snook, "From Purpose to Impact."

Then, as Tanaka said, "Memorize and recite your purpose at least daily like an affirmation to help focus and drive you to accomplish what matters most in your one very brief and precious life."

CHAPTER 5

STORYTELLING

———

"Until the day we die, we are living the story of our lives. And, like a novel in process, our life stories are always changing and evolving, being edited, rewritten, and embellished by an unreliable narrator."

—JONATHAN GOTTSCHALL, AUTHOR OF

THE STORYTELLING ANIMAL

Imagine this scenario: You're fired from a job you loved after thirty years. How do you describe it? What do you tell yourself and others? How do you handle the pain, the upset, and blow to your ego?

Rita faced this challenge. When people asked what she did, she explained she'd been a university counselor and planned to continue at another university. She found it easier to center her story within her old identity.

For former colleagues, she told a more upbeat story. "Because, let's face it, I was let go," she told me wistfully. "I didn't want to tell anybody that. So I made it sound more generic, like, 'They had a change of administration,' 'They made structural changes,' or what I often said, which was sort of true, is 'They did away with my department.'"

She dropped her stiff upper lip among friends and family, letting emotions of anger and sadness peek out. She found it "more difficult to act like it was OK." However, with other people who were laid off, she could lower her guard altogether. Like Rita, they were also asking, "Who am I now?"

Herminia Ibarra and Kent Lineback, in a *Harvard Business Review* article, wrote that in the beginning of a transition when the future isn't clear, you will need to "craft different stories for different possible selves (and the various audiences that relate to those selves)."[64]

People in transition aren't strangers to the identity loss Rita was feeling.

"You've been a banker, human resource specialist, salesperson, electrician, lawyer, whatever for a long time," Marci Alboher,

---

64   Herminia Ibarra and Kent Lineback, "What's Your Story?"

career and workplace trends expert, wrote in her book *The Encore Career.* "So expect to feel strange when you leave an identity behind and no longer have an easy way to describe yourself. You may also start feeling like what some have come to call a PIP (previously important person)."[65]

Creating a story—or revising the one you've told—can help you accept your transition and see its best features. Years ago, I attended a singles event after a job loss, and I told a man there that I was out of work. He instinctively knew how to frame my story, and when he introduced me to a few people, he graciously mentioned that I was in transition and seeking a new career. By positioning my loss as an opportunity, he buoyed my spirits and helped me see how the words I chose to tell my story could change how I saw myself and was seen.

Stories shape our lives. Typically, getting to know someone includes sharing stories of how you grew up, your family dynamics, old boyfriends or girlfriends, your fears and dreams, your work life. In a transition, your story is your road map. It needs to define both who you are and where you're headed.

"Without a compelling story that lends meaning, unity, and purpose to our lives, we feel lost and rudderless," wrote Ibarra and Lineback.[66] "We need a good story to reassure us that our plans make sense—that, in moving on, we are not discarding everything we have worked so hard to accomplish

---

65 Marci Alboher, *The Encore Career Handbook.* (9)
66 Herminia Ibarra and Kent Lineback, "What's Your Story?"

and selfishly putting family and livelihood at risk. It will give us motivation and help us endure frustration, suffering, and hard work."

STORIES FOR RENEWAL

For Nicolas Babin, who we met in the preface, two stories helped him rise from the depths of despair. One was a motto he had heard while working in Japan: Fall seven times, get up eight.

"When everything's fine, you don't think about anything else. Then suddenly you have this grain of salt that goes into your life and stops everything," said Babin. "And so you have two options. One is to give up, the other to get up again. Always get up one more time than you've fallen."

Babin's other story showed that failure isn't fatal. He had to digitize chemical factories in China where he had never worked before and even though he knew nothing about chemicals. "I thought then, 'You will learn, and the worst case is that you fail.' And that spirit helped me a lot during this time."

Rita's story smacked up against people's expectations. At age seventy-one, people assumed she was living the retired good life. "Sometimes it's easy to go with the flow and say, 'Oh, yeah, it's great. I'm volunteering. I'm taking a class,'" she said. "It's not like I'm thirty years old, and if you said you're not working, the response would be 'Oh, how are you looking for another job? I'll help you.' If you're in your seventies, people don't think you need or want to work."

As Rita's story has evolved, she has become more lighthearted. It's difficult to say which came first — her new story or her attitude.

"I feel like people are sick of hearing my stories and my struggles. So sometimes my story has changed to make it sound better than it is, because I want to project a more positive image," she said, and then paused. "But it has changed. I am more used to being home, to working part-time. And I'm volunteering. It's a better story. It's not so focused on having lost the job or being let go from the job. It's past that. It's more like, 'What am I doing now?' and less about what I did in the past or what happened."

WHAT IS A STORY?

We were all weaned on once-upon-a-time stories that transported us to far off places with heroes and heroines and dastardly devils. Good stories are a balm to our soul, letting us empathize with characters' ups and downs.

"Stories are the pathway to engaging our right brain and triggering our imagination," wrote psychologist Pamela Rutledge. "By engaging our imagination, we become participants in the narrative. We can step out of our own shoes, see differently, and increase our *empathy* for others. Through imagination, we tap into creativity that is the foundation of self-discovery and change."[67]

---

67   Pamela Rutledge, "The Psychological Power of Storytelling."

In their *Harvard Business Review* article, Ibarra and Line-back wrote about a networking event of senior managers who were downsized from lucrative jobs. Unfortunately, most of the managers, in sharing what they had done, simply recounted a laundry list of credentials and jobs. Some even stated their place of birth. As a result, the audience didn't care, because they weren't clear on how to help.[68]

The senior managers in Ibarra and Lineback's example failed to distinguish between facts and a story. The writer E. M. Forster brilliantly explained the difference using two similar stories. Here's the first story: "The king dies and then the queen died." Here's the second story: "The king dies and then the queen died because of grief."[69] The first story doesn't touch you. The second tugs at your heartstrings.

Older people often resemble Ibarra and Lineback's senior managers in their factual recitals, while younger people are more likely to be emotional. Arruda, the personal branding expert, explained a younger and older person's different modes of storytelling. The younger person might start, "'I am passionate about data analysis. Finding the meaning in a series of numbers intrigues me.' An older person might say, 'Having spent twenty-four years in data analytics, I have been able to accomplish x, y, and z.'" Arruda advises, "Tell me a story that will make me care."

---

68 Herminia Ibarra and Kent Lineback, "What's Your Story?"
69 "E. M. Forster: The Difference Between Story and Plot."

CREATING BELIEVABLE STORIES

Bear in mind, stories can't be strung together willy-nilly. Instead, they must be constructed logically to be believable. "All good stories have a characteristic so basic and necessary it's often assumed," said Ibarra and Lineback. "That quality is coherence, and it's crucial to life stories of transition." If a story is meaningful, the past is related to the present and the present provides a window to the future."[70]

"Coherence is crucial to a life story of transition because it is the characteristic that most generates the listener's trust," said Ibarra and Lineback. "If you can make your story of change and reinvention seem coherent, you will have gone far in convincing the listener that the change makes sense for you and is likely to bring success—and that you're a stable, trustworthy person."

Reinvention stories don't rise out of thin air.

"While the concept of 'reinvention' is tantalizing (think: "fresh slate," "unrealized dreams," etc.), most people don't construct a new career from scratch at midlife," wrote Nancy Collamer, author, speaker, and semi-retirement expert. "The stories you read about—the accountant turned cattle rancher, or the doctor turned vineyard owner—make for great press, but they are the exception, not the norm. In reality, most people choose a second-act career that is in some small way, shape, or form related to what they did before."[71]

---

70   Herminia Ibarra and Kent Lineback, "What's Your Story?"
71   Nancy Collamer, "5 Strategies for Reinventing Your Career."

For example, Frederick G. Thompson, who for twenty-six years worked for and owned PR agencies, didn't create a new story when he sought a position with a nonprofit. Instead, he reshaped his story. "I had helped hundreds of large, successful corporations develop successful branding stories and propositions," he said. "And now I was bringing those skills to assist nonprofit organizations to achieve their goals.' The secret sauce to success in the nonprofit area is to learn from the for-profits."

Providing a direct link, as Thompson did, from his past to his future is essential to any cogent transition story. Clark, the Duke University professor, told me that one of the "biggest pitfalls" she's seen is that people don't connect the dots between their past, present, and future. "They will say, 'I used to do this, and now I do that.' And that is fine. It's not inaccurate, but it's not necessarily helpful. If you don't explain exactly how your skills transfer or why you should fit into something and how you're able to add value, people often just come up with weird explanations or they just sort of shrug and don't get it." Connecting the past to your future will help people understand your story.

Once you've created a coherent story, you need to ensure it has another attribute—it also must engender respect. Blaming external circumstances for your situation is easy. But then you look like someone buffeted by fate. Why should someone listen to you if you can't own your story?

Ibarra and Lineback remind us that "it's not wise to base the reasons for transformation primarily outside ourselves. 'I got fired' may be a fact we must explain and incorporate into our stories, but it's rarely recognized as a good justification for seeking whatever we're seeking. External reasons tend to create the impression that we simply accept our fate."[72]

Clark shared an example of how to tell a story linking past to present while assuming responsibility for your career. "I was an attorney for thirty years, and I've now transitioned into nonprofit management. I have seen that the legal system was not properly serving the most vulnerable people, and I decided that this was a great opportunity for me to use my skills to give back to the profession."

> If a story is meaningful, the past is related to the present and the present provides a window to the future.

STORIES EVOLVE OVER TIME

Grace, who we met in Chapter 2, needed a cooling-off period after losing her job before she could tell her story. First, she had to deal with her distress and get her bearings.

"I did not feel good. I was upset and disappointed that I didn't get to do the things that I knew we were capable of doing had we had a supportive CEO. So I felt blunted in my role."

---

72 Herminia Ibarra and Kent Lineback, "What's Your Story?"

She needed to give herself permission to reflect rather than act on impulse or emotion.

Taking time for self-analysis paid off in an aha moment. Coaching, mentoring, and teaching had always been a part of her career and something she enjoyed. But they were minor notes, not the dominant soundtrack of her career.

She asked herself, "'Why don't I figure out how to make that a more major part of my job?' Learning. Adult education. I had been toying with that in my mind in prior years, but now the pieces fit. The story fit. And I was like *wow*. I felt good about it. This does make sense. The pieces do hang together."

While epiphany moments are staples of career reinvention stories, Ibarra in another *Harvard Business Review* article cautioned that these moments of truth are less the cause of a reinvention and more the understanding of changes that have been brewing.[73] In Grace's case, she had been playing different roles in her mind for months.

While Grace was clearer on what she wanted to do, the path to getting there wasn't yet visible.

"I don't mind figuring out how to get somewhere," she said. "But I would like to know where I'm going, and without having that thing that I was aiming for, I was a little bit lost. So when I could focus on an idea, it became clear."

---

73   Herminia Ibarra, "How to Stay Stuck in the Wrong Career."

Having her bearings, she could then ask herself what classes or certificates to take to compensate for any knowledge gaps and what people to talk with to pinpoint opportunities. Suddenly, what had seemed to be a closed world opened up.

Grace's story has evolved. Where originally she offered a buffet of her skills and asked for feedback from people she networked with, she now talks about how her social science background, her understanding of people, her communications skills, and her joy in turning "lightbulbs on in people," all make her a good business educator.

Psychologist, author, and professor Cecilia Dintino cited Northwestern University psychologist Dan McAdams and his concept of stories comprising our "narrative identity." Dintino wrote, "We don't live one story or one identity. Instead, this narrative of self is ongoing, always integrating the latest information and developing into something new."[74]

While Grace's story was becoming clearer, it wasn't yet complete. She wanted to flesh it out so people would understand her desire to head in a new direction. "What my story is and what I would like it to be are not the same thing," she mused. "I still feel like I have more to fill in. Being hard on myself, I feel I'm a little bit stuck in this exploration phase. I'm impatient with myself about being able to make the transition." To help her move on, she planned to hire a career coach.

---

74 Cecilia Dintino, "Re-Story Your Life."

Grace's experience wasn't atypical. "Nearly everyone who tries to figure out a next career takes a long time to find the one that is truly right," wrote Ibarra. "Most career transitions take about three years. It is rarely a linear path: We take two steps forward and one step back, and where we end up often surprises us."[75]

In her book *Reinventing You*, Clark quoted Henry Wadsworth Longfellow on perception. "We judge ourselves by what we feel capable of doing while others judge us by what we in fact have already done." Clark explained how people find it difficult to understand a dramatic career reinvention. "So when you're a finance guy who moves into marketing or a venture capitalist who wants to become a career coach or an executive trying to win a promotion, your pathway may make perfect sense to you, but that doesn't mean it's clear to everyone else."[76] That's why if you are changing careers, you need to craft a clear, easy-to-understand, logical story.

I remember many moons ago interviewing for jobs following my MBA program and the astonished reaction of recruiters. I had previously been a social worker and journalist, and when I mentioned these prior careers, proud of my accomplishments, the recruiters wrote me off as someone without a defined career path. Granted, those were the days when people didn't easily switch careers. I still think it would be a hard sell today. After the reaction I received, I removed my

---

75 Ibid.
76 Dorie Clark, Reinventing You: Define Your Brand, Imagine Your Future. (3)

social work degree and experience from my resumé to offer a more coherent story. After doing so, I secured some job offers. While it all made perfect sense to me, I couldn't get anyone else to understand. I don't suggest lying about your career path. But sometimes artful editing can help.

While Grace knew she could return to a marketing role and her job search would quickly end, she didn't want that resolution.

"I just feel done with that," she said matter-of-factly. "It's not what I really want to do. I don't want to be in a situation where I have to do this."

She was caught in that squirmy in-between space between what she was and what she wants to be. "There's got to be a better way in the world to take experienced, mid-career, late-career professionals and reorient. That to me is the missing link."

To find that link, she revisited her resumé, thinking about how she could enhance her story. "Instead of just looking for work, why don't I just do some work?" she told herself. She volunteered as the director of educational development for a nonprofit advocating for women 50+ in the workplace. That boosted her confidence to do something new. "It's not an employee job, per se, but at least it's a project that I could put in my portfolio and say, 'I did this from soup to nuts. I made this plan. I created these educational opportunities.'"

We judge ourselves by what we feel capable of doing while others judge us by what we in fact have already done.

PRACTICE MAKES PERFECT

Like any performance, a story gets better in the retelling. Don't expect to have a great story off the bat. "Any veteran storyteller will agree that there's no substitute for practicing in front of a live audience," wrote Ibarra and Lineback. "Tell and retell your story; rework it like a draft of an epic novel until the right version emerges."[77]

"I tell people to practice their story in phone calls," said Sree Sreenivasan, Marshall R. Loeb visiting professor of digital innovation at Stony Brook University School of Journalism and the social media guru we met in the introduction. "Why should people listen to you? If you can't tell your own story, how can I believe you would be good at telling my story and my company's story?"

"You'll know you've honed your story when it feels both comfortable and true to you," wrote Ibarra and Lineback. "But you cannot get there until you put yourself in front of others—ultimately, in front of strangers—and watch their faces and body language as you speak."

---

77 Herminia Ibarra and Kent Lineback, "What's Your Story?"

A career story's power is reinforced with examples and proof points. Grace planned to create a resource kit to showcase her volunteer work. She recognized that she had to sing her own song louder.

"Maybe I haven't pumped myself up enough," she said. "Maybe I've been too demure to really go out there boldly with what I feel is a thin amount of experience in this arena."

Don't be afraid to tell your own story assertively and with gusto. Otherwise, you risk others misinterpreting, and even misunderstanding, your story.

How do you put your best foot forward when you tell your story? In the next chapter, we will discuss the next principle of reinvention and personal branding: crafting a personal brand.

STORYTELLING CHEAT SHEET
Here are the five keys to good storytelling:

- Initially, when what you want to do is not clear, craft different stories for different audiences.
- Connect the dots linking your past to your future aspirations.
- Create a story that's logical yet engaging. Show some passion.
- Enhance your story through volunteering and creating a resource kit.
- Practice. Practice. Practice your story.

YOUR TURN

What story have you been telling? How can you improve your story and make people care? How can you weave a coherent story, tying your past accomplishments to what you want to do moving forward? Can you tell it with passion and emotion?

CHAPTER 6

PERSONAL BRANDING

"Be yourself. Everyone else is already taken."

—OSCAR WILDE

If you can have multiple reincarnations in a lifetime, I have done so. Over my forty-five-year working life, I've been a social worker, a newspaper reporter, a marketer, and a PR entrepreneur. You could have snapped a picture of me throughout my life, and I would have not only looked different but also would have struck a new pose. I was searching for something but didn't quite know what it was. Instead of digging deep roots, I flitted from one career to another without finding a permanent home.

For a reinvention to succeed, it needs to be grounded in personal branding. Otherwise, you're like a butterfly that has only half molted. Your wings aren't properly affixed.

Personal branding is a term that gets bandied about, sometimes carrying a negative connotation. Some mistake it as marketing hype, buffing ordinary accomplishments into marvels.

In fact, personal branding is based on introspection, not puffery. As personal branding expert William Arruda told me, "It's about getting really clear about who you are. And then using that knowledge to carve a path that will help you succeed in whatever you want to do. It's aligning who you are with what you want to do and how you do it."

I'm a long-time convert to personal branding. In 1997, working in communications and PR, I stumbled across an article in *Fast Company* by Tom Peters that changed my life. The article was a manifesto for personal branding. "To be in business today, our most important job is to be head marketer for the brand called You," Peters proclaimed. "You're every bit as much a brand as Nike, Coke, or Pepsi."[78]

Peters' words rang true to me. I followed them to some extent with my own PR agency. When I hung out my shingle some twenty-five years ago, I was simply Ms. PR; later, I became Ms. Tech PR, providing services exclusively to technology companies. And after the dot-com meltdown of the first decade of the twenty-first century, I morphed into a B2B PR expert,

---

78   Tom Peters, "The Brand Called You."

targeting companies selling their wares to other businesses, not consumers. It was my calling card and specialization. I was not just a run-of-the-mill PR person but a B2B PR expert.

Along the way, I modified Peters' approach for my clients. In the B2B space, it's called *thought leadership*, but it resembles personal branding. Through positioning and messaging, a no-name executive was transformed into an authority. Clients were quoted in the media, speaking at trade shows, and authoring articles. Thanks to thought leadership, an unknown person became an industry icon.

However, thought leadership, while effective, was personal branding lite. It omitted the introspection necessary for a true reinvention. For that, you need to peel away all the extraneous parts of your self-image to reach your core. Sure, you might be good at sales, but what is behind that? What makes you tick? Is it your amazing people skills? Your communications talents? Your fear of failure? Ultimately, personal branding requires turning a scope on yourself and looking hard.

PERSONAL BRANDING REQUIRES SHEDDING OLD SKILLS AND ADDING NEW ONES

Think of personal branding as subtraction and addition. First you scrape away the excess—what's no longer relevant or holding you back. Though it's difficult to admit, I'm ready to relinquish some of my PR responsibilities. They're shackling me from taking new steps. Additionally, I want to add some new skills to my repertoire, including coaching.

Writing this book has helped me reframe the way I see myself, letting me integrate my different talents for my next act. Upon the book's publication, I plan to be a personal branding and reinvention coach for people 50+, combining my social work, marketing, and PR skills. Currently, I'm in the trenches doing my own reinvention and rebranding.

Consequently, I know how essential personal branding is to reinventing yourself. Acting as both a shining light and armor, it distinguishes you in a sea of competitors while protecting you when you hit the inevitable career bump. As Dorie Clark, the reinvention expert, wrote, "If there are layoffs or cutbacks at your company, being recognized in your field makes it far more likely that you'll be snapped up quickly by another firm." Or at least you'll be better positioned for your next act.[79]

Personal branding, of course, is not simply the prerogative of people 50+. In fact, if you have worked with millennials or have millennial-age children, you know that many are personal branding maestros, effortlessly sharing their lives and accomplishments on social media. That self-promotion ease, however, doesn't come naturally to most boomers.

For example, consider the story of Lesley Jane Seymour, who was a personal branding newbie when at age forty-nine she was abruptly fired from her job as editor in chief of *Marie Claire*. She had no personal brand apart from her editor role.

---

79   Dorie Clark, "How Women Can Develop—and Promote—Their Personal Brand."

Stripped of her identity, she suffered a "crippling devastation and depression."

"Talking about myself twenty-four seven was widely unappealing," Seymour wrote on LinkedIn. "Facebook was only a stomping ground for teens."[80]

Fast forward to 2016 when Seymour, at age fifty-nine, relived her firing when *More* magazine was shuttered. She had been its editor in chief since 2008. But her experience this time differed. She had learned her lesson well and knew how to brand herself. Now a solid member of the digital age, Seymour "snapped a photo of the last hours of her staff and posted it" to her personal Facebook, Twitter, and LinkedIn. Not alone, she had instant access to a supportive network.

"Hundreds of friends, competitors, and readers jumped in to say how sad and angry they were that a magazine of such intelligence and quality was being shuttered," she said. Instead of feeling isolated, she felt "embraced by an incredibly nurturing and giving community."[81] When she left *More*, over six hundred loyal readers posted on social media, encouraging her to "reach higher, not to give up," and to strike out on her own. One even offered seed funding for her next project. "Instead of crippling devastation and depression, I found hope and a sense of renewal," she said.[82]

---

80 Lesley Jane Seymour, 2016. "The Joys of Losing Your Job in the Digital Age."

81 Ibid.

82 Ibid.

This time she had the resources to grow her personal brand. "Day after day, I posted stories to social media (personal to Facebook, business to LinkedIn, trends to Twitter) and tweaked them to see which created the most traction," she said. "I added my social handles to my email signatures and business cards. I jettisoned my obscure Pradagirl47 handle (given to me in a fit of 'for God's sake, just pick something, woman!' pique by my nine-year-old daughter) in favor of an easy-to-identify proper name. I attended every networking event—and every lunch—I was invited to."[83]

Seymour had shed the comfort of her editorial cocoon and learned to embrace social media and networking. She exemplifies how to develop new skills like social media and networking to build your brand. Similarly, I have branded myself on social media—in my case as a B2B PR expert. People expect me to post content about that. Through social media, I've connected with friends and colleagues who care about the subject, some of whom I've met offline. And now as I transition to personal branding and reinvention, I have begun to post content on those subjects. While it's comforting to stay in one place, it's antithetical to personal branding and reinvention.

Think of personal branding as subtraction and addition. First you scrape away the excess—what's no longer relevant or holding you back.

83   Ibid.

PERSONAL BRANDING IS DELIVERING VALUE AND PACKAGING WHAT YOU DO

Once upon a time, you didn't have to think about a personal brand. The typical person worked for a company for life, retiring with the proverbial gold watch and a tidy pension. Today, however, the average person isn't tied to one company and typically has many years after age fifty or even sixty-five to continue to work and contribute.

As you age, you think about yourself differently and develop new skills. Yet your new self-image isn't enough to get you hired. You need to package yourself, so people know what you do and want to engage with you. That packaging is brand-ing—a form of selling and marketing yourself.

Let's say, for example, that you want to reinvent yourself as a yoga teacher as Judy Freedman did. Freedman had taken early retirement at age fifty-five from her job as the director of global communications at Campbell Soup Company. Besides adjusting to her jobless status, she was coping with the loss of her husband four years before, and as part of her healing process, she discovered mindfulness, meditation, and yoga.

"I liked the physical aspects of yoga as well as the mental and spiritual," she told me. "It kept me focused on the present."

Already a blogger, she added yoga teacher to her portfolio and, after getting accredited, rebranded herself as a part-time yoga instructor. She created business cards, reached out to local recreational facilities, and because she was passionate and knowledgeable, developed a following. In Freedman's case, she had money saved so she didn't have the financial worries that plague so many older people.

She used her years of communications skills to become a relatable yoga teacher, taking time to choreograph her classes and choose the right music and poems or quotations. She targeted older students seeking a gentler routine. She also started training to become a Reiki master so she could offer more restorative practices to her students. By learning new skills and networking, she launched her new identity as a yoga instructor.

At the same time, she continued to blog, expanding her initial focus on travel to talking about lifestyle issues for boomer women such as the need to slow down.

Freedman illustrates how you can act your way into a new brand. You don't wake up in the morning and become a brand. "People think their brand is their company," said Sree Sreenivasan. "But your company is not your brand. It's what you do that's your brand." And it is how people perceive those activities.

DISCOVERING YOUR BRAND
You already have a brand of some sort—your reputation. As Jeff Bezos, the CEO of Amazon, famously said, "Your brand is what people say about you when you are not in the room."[84]

---

84 Anna Rogers, "What Are People Saying About Your Brand When You're Not in the Room?"

To understand how you're perceived, Clark suggested doing what she calls a three-word exercise. This involves asking four to six people (friends and colleagues who know you well) to describe you in three words, the top-of-mind words they associate most strongly with you.

Clark's exercise shines a light on your brand. "By the time you get four or five or six people weighing in, you are almost certainly going to see commonalities in what they say about you," said Clark. "And that begins to give you clues to the traits or the skills that are seen by a broad swath of people as being most unique about you." It's a quick read on how others see you.

Similarly, Thompson, the PR agency executive turned non-profit head who we met in Chapter 1, recommended talking to friends and associates about how they perceive your brand.

"True, you might think you know yourself," said Thompson. "But often, friends and associates will provide new insights into your persona that you never considered . . . or never appreciated."

As you're seeking feedback, look inward. "Ask yourself," said Arruda, "'What makes you different? How do you distinguish yourself from competitors? What are your strengths? Your passions? Your skills? Your challenges? What message about yourself do you want to tell?'"

Don't expect to go "mirror, mirror, on the wall, what is my personal brand?" and have it reflected back. Instead, a useful way to understand your brand is to do what Thompson calls a skills inventory, assessing both your hard and soft skills. Hard skills are those needed to fulfill a position's requirements. If, for example, you're a realtor, you're knowledgeable about sales transactions law. Soft skills are interpersonal skills such as communication, relationship-building, and customer service. A real estate agent, for instance, might need to be an excellent listener and relationship builder.

A skills inventory provides insight into future opportunities. "You're not going to suddenly become a television repair person," said Thompson. "You don't have to go through this really painful reinvention process that probably wouldn't work anyway. But you have a whole lot of general skills that can be applied to lots of different situations." A skills inventory template from Thompson is included in the resource guide at the book's conclusion.

Thompson's own story exemplifies the power of recasting your skills. At age fifty-five, he moved from the for-profit to nonprofit world. He repackaged himself as a "senior operating executive with skills in marketing, fundraising, and operations," which he calls "the trinity of things nonprofits need to succeed." He wrote articles for nonprofit outlets on marketing subjects and also spoke on the subject at conferences. He was hired by a nonprofit in less than twelve months.

Personal branding takes time, exploration, and, perhaps, significant rethinking. That was the case for Jeff Sheehan, who at age fifty-six was downsized from his sales executive job with a Japanese electronics company, since unless you're at the director level, VP level, or above, Sheehan's old employer considered you dispensable. Sheehan learned that "it's incumbent that people magnify to the hilt what they do. Beware of being a generalist but develop a skill that aligns with what's popular in your area of expertise and what's in high demand."

Sheehan, who had been active on social media, transformed himself into a social media marketing consultant and speaker. However, because practically anyone with a pulse can call himself a social media or marketing expert, he found it hard to get paid gigs.

Sheehan's experience demonstrates that you can do everything right, but if there isn't demand for your work and if you're not seen as a specialist, you won't go far. He found that within marketing and social media, those who prospered concentrated on an area such as websites, pay per click, Facebook ads, or video marketing. Succeeding as a generalist was tough. In Sheehan's case, he was content with the occasional paid gig and volunteer work.

One way to help ensure your personal branding takes off is to do a branding exercise. Just as companies do branding reviews, so can individuals.

That's what Frenchman Nicolas Babin did to brand himself, applying the same rigor he had used to brand products as the director of corporate communications for Sony Europe. He thought about how to position himself in twenty-five, fifty, and one hundred words, and asked himself, "Who was Nicolas Babin?"

Babin created a brand document that included a vision, mission, positioning, brand story, and brand plan. I've included a copy of Babin's latest brand strategy document in the resource section at the book's end. While Babin's document is comprehensive and may be beyond what you need, consider it a starting point for your branding exercise. You may want to cut it to include only your vision, mission, positioning, and goals. Those four items will ensure that you have a path to follow. Don't stint on these exercises. Together, they will give you the structure to assess and develop your brand.

CREDENTIALS AREN'T ENOUGH

People fifty and up often forget one other element to personal branding. As simple as it sounds, it's being likable. Often people over fifty, according to Arruda, are so focused on making themselves believable that they forget about being engaging.

"Older professionals work on the credibility piece a lot," he said. "'Look at me, I've accomplished this. I've had these roles. I've saved the company this much money. I have these degrees. I've worked at these five important companies.' All those things make you credible, but they leave out the likability piece. Why would somebody want to work with you?

What makes you human? How can I connect with you on a deeper, more emotional level?"

And part of humanizing your brand is making it relatable. It's not enough to draw a line between what you were and your future career. Your brand also needs to make sense to people you're trying to reach. Those who do this successfully translate their work into the right lingo. Rita, in her new incarnation, emphasized the counseling part of her background, even though it had been a minor part of her past work. Instead of using the words *academic advisor,* she highlighted her counseling experience. "It's translating your work into the terminology that's appropriate for the field you want to go into," she said. "It's like translating from English to French."

Realistically, it's easy to mistake personal branding for chest thumping and ego gratification. As Arruda told me, "One of the biggest misconceptions people have about personal branding is that it's about telling people how great you are." Instead, he said, "It's about delivering value, about generosity in sharing your ideas and point of view."

As you give freely to others, you're shaping your brand. While you don't want to boast, you do want to put your best foot forward. That means tying loose ends together into an attractive whole.

Many people over age fifty aren't accustomed to thinking about packaging themselves. They have a resumé and sterling credentials and believe that's enough. However, if you want to position yourself for success, you need props. Stacey Ross Cohen, a personal branding blogger, speaker, and CEO of a public relations and marketing agency, said it's akin to creating a tool kit. Your "kit" will contain your resumé or bio, a photo, and examples of your work. "Make sure every word counts and your value comes through," Cohen said. Consider it your visual representation of your brand.

> Part of humanizing your brand is making it relatable. It's not enough to draw a line between what you were and your future career. You also need to make it understandable.

LIVING YOUR BRAND

Now that you know the components of personal branding, how do you put your own brand into practice? How do you ensure the image you're projecting is the one you want? Let's discuss the two keys to doing so: content creation and evaluation.

A personal branding strategy isn't complete without doing what Clark calls, "living your brand," or building it through content creation. This is not a one-and-done exercise but ongoing.

"Market yourself in your target industry as a thought leader by filling the content gap," advised Thompson. "The demand for content these days is so strong that most industry conferences and local civic and charity groups such as Rotary or Kiwanis have an urgent need for speakers and panelists," who are selected based on their content and expertise.

Similarly, Joe Pulizzi, author, speaker, and founder of the Content Marketing Institute, said, "Focus on a content niche where you can be the leading expert in the world on that particular topic."[85]

Of course, you won't become an industry authority by writing or posting one article. Consistency matters. Otherwise, people can easily think your new interest is a passing fad. By sharing content often, either work you create or curate, Clark said people will notice and say, "'For the past year, she's been sharing these articles. I guess this is real. This is really her thing now.'" By frequently writing and posting on one subject, you've branded yourself an industry expert.

Remember though that a personal brand isn't preserved in aspic. Think of it as a living, breathing entity that evolves as your business or career changes. "You don't just build your brand and say, 'Branding done, time to move on to the next thing,'" said Arruda. "Regularly check in and ask yourself, 'Is it still working? Am I still happy doing what I'm doing? Are the people that I'm competing with the same? Or do I need to think about that differently?' If people are willing to ask themselves those questions, they'll be in a

---

85 "51 Personal Branding Quotes: Powerful Advice You Can't Miss."

really good place to keep their brand relevant and not find out that all of a sudden the world's moved on, and they haven't moved with it."

For example, Babin ensured his brand stayed relevant by evaluating it every six months. His mission—to help companies in digital transformation—was his north star guiding his work. While his mission remained firm, his goals and tactics changed. "The first year, I wanted to have ten happy customers across Europe," he explained. "Now, I have about twenty-five customers around the world. So things are changing constantly. But they are small points compared to knowing what my positioning and mission is." His branding exercise had given him stability with flexibility.

If you don't brand yourself, someone else will. You'll be perceived a certain way whether you want to be or not. By branding yourself, however, you're ensuring you're seen in your own image. No longer just a participant in your life, you've become its director.

PERSONAL BRANDING CHEAT SHEET

As a handy reminder, here are the key strategies for personal branding:

- **Introspection:** Who are you? Do Clark's three-point exercise and a skills inventory.

- **Creating your brand:** What is your vision, mission, positioning, and goals? Do Babin's branding exercise in the resource guide.
- **Packaging your brand:** What is your elevator pitch—a summary of yourself short enough to say on an elevator ride? How do you make it resonate for people in your target audience?
- **Humanizing your brand:** How do you make your brand likable and relatable?
- **Delivering your brand:** How can you showcase your brand? What kind of content can you create? How can you get your name and expertise known?

Now that you know why personal branding is essential, let's look at our last principle: social media and mentoring.

YOUR TURN

How would you define your personal brand? How do you want it to evolve? After some introspection from using the personal branding cheat sheet, describe your brand and what you want it to become. Write your elevator pitch. Rewrite it and rewrite it until it resonates.

CHAPTER 7

SOCIAL MEDIA AND MENTORING

—

"No longer do we have to rely on word of mouth. Instead, a new, profound type of empowerment comes with sharing via LinkedIn, Twitter, and a personal blog."

–DORIE CLARK, REINVENTION EXPERT,

AUTHOR, AND PROFESSOR

Why do some people seem to be reinvention magicians? One minute they're virtually unknown, and the next they're seemingly everywhere—overnight sensations and internet stars. While reinvention may seem to happen in a flash, hidden is the toil and hard work that preceded it. Reinvention and personal branding don't happen in a vacuum—or a day. Key to getting any reinvention to fly are outside resources such as social media and mentoring. Think of them as the propeller to your reinvention—what helps it soar. Let's look at each of these, starting with social media. Together with the other six principles of reinvention and rebranding, they will ensure your next act succeeds.

SOCIAL MEDIA IS YOUR BEST FRIEND

Doubtless, you know the types. One person is so fearful of appearing old that he posts a picture of himself on social media that's at least twenty years old. One is social media–phobic, so skittish about being online and proudly proclaiming she wants nothing to do with it. Another person has only a baby toe in, posting once in a while when the mood hits. And yet another is the rabid poster, updating his profile furiously and posting a new video every hour. I'm sure you have your own favorite caricatures. I too plead guilty to my share of online faux pas. Social media goofs, however, haven't stopped me. And they shouldn't stop you.

While it's easy to poke fun at online behavior and say, "It's not my thing," social media is an essential tool for anyone over fifty who wants to reinvent himself or herself. In fact, according to Dorie Clark, "It's even more critical for older people to have a social presence because it's increasingly viewed as a proxy for staying current professionally."[86]

---

86 Dorie Clark, "How to Reinvent Yourself After 50."

Still, older people hesitate to venture online. In fact, Keith Keller, the Twitter maestro, found that older people who grew up before computers didn't get his fascination with being online. They simply wanted to talk with "real people" in a physical place.

Listening to Keller's friends, you might think that social media is a foreign country that takes a lot of work to get to. As William Arruda noted, "I think there are a lot of misconceptions about social media. One of the reasons older people are reluctant to be on the web is because they think it takes forever, that digital branding is time-consuming. It actually doesn't take that much time. Nine minutes a day of social media interaction can be enough to have an impact yet is certainly not too onerous."

Think of spending nine minutes a day as exercising your social media muscle. It will help shore up your reinvention. Today, social media is your megaphone, letting you share your message with the world, get feedback, and begin conversations. As the storied *New Yorker* cartoon facetiously said, "No one knows you're a dog online." In fact, anyone can start posting engaging content and attracting a following.

Today, social media is your megaphone, letting you share your message with the world, get feedback, and begin conversations.

Indeed, social media is an ideal platform to forge a personal brand and identity. As Clark said in an interview, "No longer do we have to rely on word of mouth. Instead, a new, profound type of empowerment comes with sharing via LinkedIn, Twitter, and a personal blog."[87]

Using social media, you can present yourself as a subject matter expert, posting and sharing useful content. You don't have to be an all-out authority—just know a little more than the next person. Over the years, I've turned myself into a B2B PR and marketing expert online by blogging and being active on LinkedIn and Twitter. Most of the content I post pertains to PR and marketing. Now that I am pivoting toward reinvention and personal branding, I have started posting content in those areas.

You may be wondering what you will talk about. But you have a lifetime of resources to draw upon. As career expert Marie Zimenoff noted, "Over the years, those over fifty have worked with many people. They have connections and a network. How can those networks support them and buoy them through their career transitions?" Zimenoff asked. "Social media can help them do that, so they stay connected with people. It's a tool for them to build some visibility, create or share content, and maintain their network and community."

Indeed, social media puts networking literally at your fingertips. Suddenly, with a few keystrokes, you can follow and

---

87 Carrie Kerpen, "Bringing Your Personal Brand to Life with Dorie Clark."

engage with industry thought leaders. While your email to a thought leader might land in the virtual trash, you can gain an expert's attention by commenting on his or her post or article. However, don't risk spreading yourself too thin by being active on too many networks. You'll end up forging relationships with no one. LinkedIn, in my experience, is the number one career site for boomers. Reinvention expert John Tarnoff calls it, "your twenty-first century resumé." Through posting in LinkedIn groups and on your own profile, you will start showcasing your smarts.

If you're still hesitant to go online, a lot of good online tutorials are available, and I've listed some of them in the resource guide following this chapter. Do what Ken Jacobs, executive coach, consultant, and trainer, did and find a reverse mentor, someone younger than you who can show you the social media ropes.

As Evan Kirstel, social media expert and cofounder of eViRa Health, told me, "So many resources are on the internet now. There's almost no excuse for not knowing how to do something. If you just go to Google and say, 'How do I create a Twitter account?' you'll find an endless number of step-by-step videos or articles to do things."

The internet is truly an inquisitive person's bonanza. Social media is easy to use and gives you worldwide reach and a platform to showcase your expertise. It morphs a liability—your little-known brand—into an advantage.

MENTORING IS YOUR SUPPORT SYSTEM

Just as it takes a village to raise a child, career reinvention requires a support system. That is where mentoring happens. Perhaps you think that after a certain age, you're too old to have a mentor. Isn't that just for new or mid-career folks? Author Daniel Pink disabuses you of that. "People are never too old to need a mentor," he said.[88]

Mentors aren't celestial beings on high but down-to-earth, experienced, trusted advisors. Susan Chadick, the CEO of Chadick Advisors, explained that a mentor is "someone who has your back." Having a mentor means you're not alone as you venture into new areas.

> People are never too old
> to need a mentor.

You've probably had mentors at key points of your life, though you might not have called them that. Nancy Collamer noted, "Think back on major transitions in your life like graduations, marriage, or new jobs. Chances are you had a network of family, friends, and mentors who guided, cheered, and supported you. Surrounding yourself with a caring community is a critical part of career reinvention success, too."[89]

---

88   Tami Kamin Meyer, "You Can Reinvent Yourself, No Matter Your Age."

89   Nancy Collamer, "How Women Can Reinvent Their Careers After 50."

Don't adopt the fallacy of thinking of a mentor as someone who satisfies all your needs. No one can do that—not even a loving spouse. Instead, think of a mentor as being part of a collective that guides you, what Chadick called your "unique advisory board." In her own life, Chadick has had multiple people help her navigate her business and other knotty issues. She had one person, a savvy investment banker, she sought for counsel on ticklish business questions. If she's disturbed about something, she reached out to a female colleague who helped her rebalance.

"I'm too old to have a mentor," she said laughingly. "I think of these people as those I turn to for advice and feedback on a variety of planes."

Besides your advisory board, you should have one person you check in with regularly, according to personal branding expert William Arruda. Consider it your way of taking the temperature of your brand. "Having someone who asks you questions is a great way to see if your brand needs some reinvention, evolution, or tweaking," said Arruda. Here are some questions, courtesy of Arruda, that your mentor might ask:

- Am I still happy doing what I'm doing?
- What struggles am I experiencing?
- Do my struggles have to do with changes?
- In my world, am I still competing against the same people?

For mentoring to work, don't consider it a one-sided relationship where you're doing all the receiving. Instead, as in any relationship, seek a mutually beneficial balance. Clark wrote, "For these relationships to endure, make sure they're reciprocal. That way, you're learning from each other rather than imposing on one another's time (or worrying that you're doing so). It can be as simple as offering to help tune up a mentor's social profile (if you're adept at that and he's expressed interest) to giving movie or book recommendations."[90] Mentoring works both ways.

But how do you find a mentor? Clark noted, "Stop looking for the 'mythical mentor' who has it all: seniority, authority, and a magnanimous desire to help you."[91] Instead, Clark advised that you consider the people you already know with skills or traits that you admire and reach out to them.

And while it's typical to think of mentoring as working with an older colleague, mentors can be any age. In fact, reverse mentoring, partnering with someone younger, can be powerful. A younger person, for example, might help you with technology or social media while you counsel him or her on business.

Beyond your own network, the internet has made it much easier to connect with people in all walks of life. Avoid the temptation, however, to hurl requests to anyone. Get to know someone first and seek ways to give, not just take. "Mentorships work best as sincere relationships where mentors and mentees are both giving and receiving," said writer David

---

90 Dorie Clark, "Your Career Needs Many Mentors, Not Just One."
91 Dorie Clark, 2013. Mentorship 2.0: How to Find the Mentor You Need.

Lumb.[92] As in any good relationship, mentorship needs to add reciprocal value.

And it comes in different shapes. One form is barter, where you exchange services. Kirstel explained, "If you're an accountant, you could find some digital guru. 'Hey, I'll do your taxes for you if you can help me with the social media thing.' Or maybe it's a company that has all the marketing chops, and you could learn about digital and social marketing, but the company needs a writer and you write really well. 'You teach me all about this web and digital stuff, and I'll write for you for free.' I think there's still a lot of value in bartering and learning that way." Reciprocity is built naturally into the barter relationship.

In addition to being a mentee, don't forget about serving as a mentor yourself, where you bring your lifetime of hard-earned skills to help someone else. "Mentoring is a wonderful opportunity for people who are older to find their own sense of purpose and learn a lot about life and themselves through being present for someone younger," said Tarnoff. "The most amazing experiences I have continue to be the work that I do with my grad students in the Carnegie Mellon program, who are just at the very early stages of their careers and exploring, and I am getting so much joy out of working with them. Seeing them discover themselves is powerful and so affirming."

---

92   David Lumb, "Why You Need a Different Mentor at Every Step in Your Career."

Ideally, you will be both a mentor and a mentee—helping others while learning yourself.

A FEW THINGS TO KEEP IN MIND

- Spend nine minutes a day on social media. That's all you need to do.
- Establish yourself as an expert on social media through original and curated content.
- Have multiple mentors or advisors. No one person can satisfy all your needs.
- Give. Don't just ask when you reach out to a potential mentor.

YOUR TURN

If you're just getting started on social media, what people in your field do you admire? Start following them and share what they post. What type of content can you post to help brand yourself? If you lack your own content, curate content you like by adding your brief opinion to someone else's content. Don't overthink social media. It's meant to be quick and conversational, not a labored exercise. Regarding mentors, where do you need help? Create a checklist of areas where you need assistance, such as branding or social media. And include a list of experts you already know. Who can you reach out to for support in these areas?

A FEW FINAL WORDS

This brings us to the formal end of this book. I hope it has inspired you to dig deep and ask yourself the existential question: What can I do next? Reinventing yourself in even the smallest way can feel scary because you're chipping away at pieces of your identity. However, a stronger, more purposeful you will emerge, ready to thrive in the decades that follow.

Don't worry about reinventing yourself in a flash. Reinvention takes time and may involve trying multiple new roles. As you saw, all the successful shape-shifters interviewed for this book were skillful at attempting something new and unafraid of failing. Their path to reinvention was not a straight line.

Keith Keller knows this well. Keller didn't overthink his next act. He and the other reinvention exemplars I interviewed know that reinvention doesn't happen by sitting on your couch and mulling over options. They're testers and tinkerers.

Similarly, you don't wake up one day and say, "Voilà, I'm reinvented." Reinvention is often the outcome of a life event— the loss of a job, the death of a spouse, becoming an empty nester. Or you may have an internal warning—a feeling of malaise that something isn't working.

While it's easy to buy into the stereotypes that people 50+ are over the hill and not as smart as young people, writing this book has shown me the tremendous resilience and talents of older people. No one demonstrates this better than Nicolas Babin, who reinvented his life after a horrific accident. Babin had resilience in spades and a staunch belief in himself. "Yes, you can," he told himself. "Anything is possible."

I won't make short shrift of the challenges of reinventing yourself at 50+—especially confronting the beast of ageism. However, by adapting the framework this book proposes—the seven principles of reinvention and personal branding—you will have the tools to thrive in your next act and beyond. As you've seen, reinvention isn't a one-time event but an ongoing process as you adapt to life's vicissitudes and your changing needs and dreams. Essential for growth and learning, reinvention paradoxically ties you to the past while moving you forward. You don't become a new person, but a better version of your past selves seasoned with new skills, moxie, and knowledge.

Know that you will not be alone on your journey. As one of the seven principles, social media and mentoring, explains, you will have a network of support online and off as you try on new roles, fumble, and get up again and again.

Consider the seven principles, your foundation to change your life

1. Having a Growth Mindset
2. Being Uncomfortable
3. Willingness to Learn
4. Finding Your Purpose
5. Storytelling
6. Personal Branding
7. Social Media and Mentoring

Together, these principles will help you build a new life with more purpose and meaning. I wish you much success on your journey. You couldn't be doing anything better for yourself. Please visit thrivingat50plus.com for additional resources. And be sure to follow me on LinkedIn (linked. com/in/wendyamarx), Twitter (@wendymarx), and Instagram (@wendyamarx).

ONE MORE THING.

Before you go, please check out the resource guide that follows. People I interviewed and other personal branding and reinvention experts kindly shared helpful tips and other materials to ensure a more successful reinvention. The materials are organized by subject matter, including careers, personal branding, networking, self-assessments, and general resources.

ABOUT THE AUTHOR

———

Wendy Marx is a marketing and branding authority who has turned virtually unknown people into icons through her PR and marketing agency. Now, as a published author, she's using her branding knowledge to show how people, at age 50+, can reinvent themselves and find more meaning and purpose. A baby boomer with multiple reinventions, holding MSW, MS and MBA degrees, she knows a career journey isn't set or over just because someone reaches a certain age or point in life.

Passionate about people's ability to slide upwards, not downwards, to the finish line, she is also an avid tennis player who works hard at being mediocre. She is a caregiver to the love of her life and a theater and art enthusiast.

RESOURCE GUIDE

—

CAREER RESOURCES

AGE-PROOFING YOUR RESUMÉ AND LINKEDIN PROFILE:
https://www.forbes.com/sites/nextavenue/2018/10/01/how-to-age-proof-your-resumé-and-linkedin-profile/#1fd60db92e24

PODCAST ON HOW TO MAKE A CAREER PIVOT AT ANY AGE:
http://bit.ly/careerconfidante100818

PODCAST ON HOW TO REPURPOSE YOUR CAREER:
http://bit.ly/careerconfidante81219

WORKING AT FIFTY-PLUS:
https://www.aarp.org/work/working-at-50-plus/?intcmp=-ftr-links-jobres-working50-ewhere

CHANGING CAREERS:

https://www.aarp.org/work/career-change/?intcmp=
ftr-links-jobres-carchnge-ewhere

STARTING A BUSINESS:

https://www.aarp.org/work/small-business/?intcmp=
ftr-links-jobres-strtbiz-ewhere

RESUMÉ ADVICE:

https://www.aarp.org/work/resumé-advisor/?intcmp=
ftr-links-jobres-resumé-ewhere

TOOLS TO HELP YOU GET BACK TO WORK:

https://www.aarp.org/aarp-foundation/our-work/income/
back-to-work-50-plus/

JOB SEARCH SITES FOR 50+:
retiredbrains.com
whatsnext.com
retirementjobs.com
workforce50.com
empoweredage.com
jobs.aarp.org

CAREERS

This section is designed to help you begin reinventing yourself. If you are seeking a new career, the skills inventory below, courtesy of Frederick G. Thompson, takes you through the process of assessing your skills, matching them to new fields, and marketing yourself. Thompson is an adjunct professor at University of Virginia Darden School of Business and founder and principal of the Communications Collaborative, a marketing and brand consultancy.

SKILLS INVENTORY AND TRANSITION ACTIVATION PROCESS

STEP ONE: SKILLS INVENTORY
The Process

Take an inventory of both hard and soft skills your current and/or past career experiences have required.

- Hard skills are directly related to fulfilling a position's requirements. For example, a truck driver would have to be proficient at operating a vehicle safely; similarly, a real estate agent would have to be knowledgeable in state property sales transaction law.

- Soft skills refer to interpersonal abilities a position might require such as communications, relationship-building, customer service, critical listening, and more. Using the previous examples, success as a truck driver might require attention to scheduling details and listening attentively to dispatch or customer instructions. Success as a realtor might require empathetic listening to client needs and an ability to forge strong customer relationships.

The inventory process is also an opportunity to evaluate what position requirements you don't enjoy or you're uncomfortable with. Remember, the job transition process is intended to help you identify and secure a new position that is not only suited to the skills you already possess but one that will be more enjoyable and fulfilling.

Intended Outcome

The goal of the inventory process is to record—or *inventory*—a list of skills and talents that will demonstrate to an employer in a new job category that you are qualified to fill a position in that category.

STEP TWO: MATCHING THE INVENTORIED SKILLS WITH A DESIRED NEW POSITION

The Process

This is not an easy process. For some individuals, it will be intuitive, but others may have a lot of uncertainty as to how or where a given skills inventory might best be applied. Following are some guidelines that will help you match skills with a desired career transition target.

- Begin by preparing a list of desired career choices or "targets." For most individuals, this won't be difficult. Most people who have been working for any length of time have already developed a list of alternative career areas they'd like to explore as time and circumstances allow. This wish list, for most career transition seekers, can and should comprise the most attractive, highest-priority transition targets.

- Consider transition careers that are at least somewhat related to previous positions you've held. For example, many for-profit executives desire to make the transition to nonprofit organizations. While the nonprofit and for-profit worlds can differ, success in both areas still depends on similar core skills such as sound management, smart strategic planning, and building strong relationships.

- Be realistic and flexible. Some targets are likely to be more attainable than others. Match your desires and skills against career transition goals that are realistically achieved without undue obstacles such as challenging new education requirements, logistically complicated geographic restrictions, or burdensome financial barriers.

- Seek objective input. During the matching process, obtain third-party input from people who know you are seeking a new job. Ideally, such individuals will be able to provide an objective analysis of the job seeker's skills and where those skills might logically fit when applied to a desired situation.

Intended Outcome

The goal of the matching process is to identify career transition targets that are both immediately accessible and realistic given a transition seeker's skills, interests, and financial position.

STEP THREE: IMPLEMENTING THE TRANSITION

The Process

Once transitioning job seekers are confident that their newly inventoried skills are aligned with the skills their new career area requires, they are ready to take the third and final step—actively seeking positions in their chosen transition field. This process is complicated, of course, since the candidate in most cases has never actually worked in the new field and must "market" his or her suitability for the new position based largely on skills carried over from previous positions. Here are some guidelines for making this important phase of the transition process more successful.

- Create a CV or resumé that communicates a clear narrative of how your skills will add value to your new career category. You need a good "story" that links the benefits of your skill set to the desired goals of the organization you seek to join.

- As part of developing your story, carefully research organizations on your target list and identify unmet needs that your skills could uniquely accommodate. The goal here is to articulate how one or more of your strongest skills could add value to an area that is critical to an employer's success. In essence, focus on how *you can solve a problem* the organization has and make it a major theme of your interview discussion.

- Consider a "try before you buy" or even offer to volunteer. Many organizations are willing to consider a trial hire, particularly if an applicant's only deficiency is industry experience—a qualification that can almost always be learned on the job.

- Market yourself in the target industry as a thought leader by filling the content gap. Most industry conferences and organizations have an urgent need for speakers and panelists to provide content. These platforms as well as social media platforms like Facebook and LinkedIn provide credible opportunities for job seekers to increase their visibility as thought leaders or experts in various skills areas. For those who are transitioning in their careers, the key is to choose a skill set that is relevant to their target industry and connect the dots. As a follow-up, send a note to influential people in the career area being targeted. Start with something like, "I thought you'd be interested . . ."

Intended Outcome
The goal of implementation is to raise awareness of the transition candidate's qualifications and get in front of targeted employers for an interview.

BRANDING EXERCISE TEMPLATE

This is a sample of a branding template provided by Nicolas Babin, president of Babin Business Consulting. Use this as a starting point that you can tweak and mold to your needs.

TWENTY-FIVE-WORD (ELEVATOR) POSITIONING STATEMENT:

Global company that provides performant services around digital expertise. Change management, digital tools usage, and expertise sharing are the three pillars of our activity.

FIFTY-WORD POSITIONING STATEMENT:

Global company that provides performant services around digital expertise. Change management, digital tools usage, and expertise sharing are the three pillars of our activity.

Customers can contact us to transform their business from box-selling to solution-selling. As part of the transformation, change management and way of working will be challenged and optimized.

ONE-HUNDRED-WORD POSITIONING STATEMENT:

Global company that provides performant services around digital expertise. Change management, digital tools usage, and expertise sharing are the three pillars of our activity.

Customers can contact us to transform their business from box-selling to solution-selling. As part of the transformation, change management and way of working will be challenged and optimized.

Babin Business Consulting is specialized in all types of industries from chemical to car makers, finance to consumer electronics, start-ups to well-established companies, and for all types of management (local or international). Whatever the business, if it needs digital, Babin Business Consulting can help.

MISSION STATEMENT AND VISION
Vision
Become the all-industry expert in digital management throughout France, then Europe, and finally the US and Japan.

- Expertise and precision in project realization
- Maximum return on investment (ROI) for our customers
- Speed of exploitation
- Autonomy, product independence, flexibility, and open structure
- Trust in the team
- Leading to customer, partner, and employee satisfaction

Mission Statement
At the heart of the digital industry, helping customers with mindset change, tools usage, process implementation, and expertise.

BRAND PROMISE

Our brand promise is TRUST. This promise is exhibited in the following ways:

- Always deliver on time and within project budgets
- Provide second-to-none service
- Be professional in everything we do at all levels of the company
- Listen to our customers
- Live up to our promises and customer expectations
- Be consistently innovative
- Be useful to an ecosystem

BRAND TRAITS AND VALUES

Brand traits and values list what the organization wants its brand to stand for—its core values and beliefs. Our brand traits and values include:

- Integrity
- Honesty
- Humanism
- Loyalty
- Respect
- Humility
- Dedication
- Implication
- Sharing
- Consistency
- Productivity
- Availability
- Ambition
- Brand Signature
- Agility and Fun
- Respect of Privacy and Trust
- Orchestration
- Real Time
- Accompaniment
- Guide
- Contemporary

BRAND STORY

In 2017, after a serious car accident, Mr. Nicolas Babin decided to start his own consultancy company—Babin Business Consulting. He provides services around digital transformation, including but not limited to gamification, marketing, communication, intercultural management, social networks, and digital marketing. Babin Business Consulting signed many customers around the globe (in Europe, the US, Asia, and Australia).

Today, more than two years later, Babin Business Consulting is up and running. Its services are being used across the world in many areas (like e-health, gamification, the chemical industry, the car industry, the building industry, and consumer electronics).

BRAND ASSOCIATIONS
Brand Name
Babin Business Consulting

Logo
The Bay Bridge in San Francisco around the globe, bridging cultures, mindsets, expertise, and tools. Blue is the color of trust.

Tagline
Reliable.Performant.Agile

Motto
Fall seven times, stand up eight.

Perceived Quality

Perceived quality is the heart of what clients are buying. It directly links to the clients' reason to buy and price sensitivity. Whether the brand is a price brand or a prestige brand, perceived quality is often one of the key differentiators.

- Our brand quality perception will be built through:
  - Voice of authority program
  - Becoming a standard through partnership with associations

- Our perceived quality can be measured through regularly scheduled client and market surveys:
  - Audit
  - Our community (LinkedIn, videos, Twitter, Facebook, blogs, and forums)
  - Feedback from customers
  - Measurement of all invites to specific events and references to our brand

Brand Loyalty

Brand loyalty is the measure of commitment a client has to the brand. Retaining customers is much less expensive than attracting new ones, so companies must find a balance in their branding efforts that build awareness and loyalty in parallel.

- Brand loyalty will be built through:
  - Community management
  - Voice of authority program
  - Always adding value to customers

- Brand loyalty will be measured by:
    - Retaining customers
    - Brand audit and check blogs and forums
    - Audits from associations
    - Invitations to events as recognized experts

BRAND AWARENESS

Brand awareness measures client perception and attitude toward a brand. Studies show that when a purchasing decision is made, familiar brands will have the edge.

- Brand awareness will be built through:
    - Community management
    - Blog and forum involvement
    - Added value events (internal and external)

- Awareness can be measured by:
    - Community involvement
    - Increased sales

BRAND ASSOCIATIONS MANAGEMENT

Brand association is the dimension that most people think of when they consider the meaning of branding. These associations would include products, a company spokesperson, a particular symbol or logo, a slogan, and finally...a personality. Through associations, a brand communicates who it is, what it does, and how it does it.

- Brand associations will be designed to work together, be used consistently, and be given enough time to have an impact. These elements will be defined and documented in the Style Guide section of the Brand Guideline book and will be used religiously by every employee. Each employee will be responsible as a brand ambassador to promote and encourage the branding process and hold each other accountable.
  - Measurement for brand association usage will be done through:
    - Quarterly audits of company materials, communications, processes, etc.
    - Voice of authority document (for example, are we invited to talk at conferences?)

* * *

PERSONAL BRANDING

Personal branding is an important part of reinvention and much more than a simple "look at me" tactic. It's how you're perceived by others and a shortcut to people understanding what you're about. Here are fifteen questions to ask yourself, provided by William Arruda, motivational speaker, author, and CEO of Reach Personal Branding, the global leader in personal branding.

FIFTEEN QUESTIONS TO UNCOVER YOUR BRAND

Branding is based in authenticity. It's not spin. It's not packaging. And it's not about creating a false image for the outside world.

You need to know yourself—truly know yourself—to build your brand. That means you must get clear on your goals, values, passions, mission, strengths, and differentiation. These questions will help you uncover your brand.

1. What do you do better than anyone else?
2. If you were to receive an award, what would it be for?
3. What's the part of your job you love the most?
4. What makes you feel most confident?
5. What do you like best about yourself?
6. What do people come to you for?
7. What are you most proud of?
8. What's the most unique or quirkiest thing about you?
9. If you won the lottery and didn't need to work, how would you spend your time?
10. What quality in others do you admire the most?
11. About what topic(s) can you talk endlessly?
12. What's your preferred form of communication?
13. What did you learn about yourself from the biggest mistake you ever made?
14. If you had to focus the rest of your life on one thing, what would it be?
15. What are the three most important elements of a life filled with joy?

* * *

So how do you get your personal brand off the ground? Here are eight tips to do just that, along with a brief introduction from Stacey Ross Cohen, CEO of Co-Communications, cofounder of College Prime, speaker, and author.

EIGHT TIPS FOR GETTING STARTED IN PERSONAL BRANDING

Many of us hit midlife and crave a career change but are stumped on how to begin. The solution: personal branding. In short, personal branding differentiates you from the crowd and is about the marketing of *you*. Although it may seem brands "just happen," those who actively craft their own brand and deliver their standout value reap many benefits—career advancement, business opportunities, and more.

Below are eight tips for getting started:

1. **Strong brands are intentional.** Start by defining yourself. Determine what you do well, what you love to do, and your identity and vision. Then own it. This all starts with a self-audit to pinpoint your purpose, strengths, values, and passion. It's essential to crystallize your uniqueness—or competitive advantage—and why you're a worthy investment. Equally important is understanding your audience: what they need, how they function, and what drives them to take action.

2. **Have an answer to "what's in it for me?"** Why should your target audience employ you? What's your value? What makes you stand out from the host of other applicants? You need to stress your value and strengths. But avoid tailoring your brand too much to the audience. Make your brand about you first.

3. **Know how to work a room.** Networking is face-to-face marketing. Don't focus on how many people you meet

networking—focus on meeting the right people. Building relationships is the core of effective networking.

4. **Stay on brand.** Maintain a consistent voice across different channels. Ensure your LinkedIn, Twitter, and other profiles are up-to-date and in harmony.

5. **Be self-aware.** Always seek feedback. Ensure your brand is clearly articulated and know how to deliver on your brand and make it grow.

6. **Create a powerful online presence.** Reputation management is key. The digital footprint one leaves across the internet is the encapsulation of his or her personal brand.

7. **Have a multichannel approach.** Your tool kit should include but not be limited to: social media, blogging, volunteer work, and speaking at industry conferences. Consider all touch points, like email, phone calls, and mailed greetings. To stand out, develop a resumé with keywords and customized infographics along with powerful business cards and headshots. And create and share content that will position you as a thought leader.

8. **Deliver on your promise.** Remember: you are the product. Gauge your brand behavior and ensure you return phone calls and emails promptly. Not delivering on promises can wreak havoc on the integrity of your personal brand.

* * *

How can you align your personal brand with your job search? Meg Guiseppi, founder of Executive Career Brand and executive job search strategist, provides five key steps to do so.

FIRST STEPS TO DEFINE YOUR PERSONAL BRAND FOR A JOB SEARCH

1. Who is your target audience?

Determine what kind of work you want to do (job position and industry). Then identify which companies and organizations will afford you the opportunity to work your passion. Determine what hiring decision makers in that field are looking for candidates.

In addition, research your target list of companies. What current challenges of theirs are you uniquely qualified to help them with?

Create your personal brand by sharing the keywords and content that will attract them. Further, find out where those decision makers hang out. Position yourself in front of them. Capture their attention and stay in their line of sight.

Most importantly, as you do the work to define your brand, keep your target employers in mind. Which qualifications of yours align with what they need?

This will lead you toward employers who are a mutual good fit. These employers will benefit the most from your expertise. They are the employers who will bring you career fulfillment.

2. What is your vision and purpose?
What is your vision for the world? How can you help the world realize your vision?

What is one world problem you would like to see solved or aspect of life you'd like to see transformed or improved? This is your vision. What role will you play in making your vision happen? This is your purpose.

3. What are your values?
Knowing your top values helps you choose employers whose values match yours. Your values are your guiding principles—things like balance, being the best, agility, calmness, challenge, decisiveness, perseverance, drive, honesty, integrity, pragmatism, sensitivity, structure, teamwork, sharing, vitality, and zeal.

4. What are your passions?
What do you most enjoy doing in your personal life and work life? Think about the activities, interests, or conversational topics that fascinate and energize you.

For instance, your passions are the things that you can't wait to get to when you wake up in the morning. The things you often talk about enthusiastically with others.

Think about how your passions converge with what you do best at work.

5. What are your top personal brand attributes?
How do you define your personality? What words do those around you (at work and elsewhere) use to describe you? How do people introduce you to others? Which personality traits define how you make things happen?

Identify three or four adjectives that best describe the value you offer. Consult a thesaurus to nail the exact words. You may describe yourself as being collaborative, resilient, forward-focused, risk-taking, connected, international, visionary, diplomatic, intuitive, precise, enterprising, ethical, genuine, or accessible.

* * *

An essential element in personal branding building is creating trust. Greg Monaco, a brand coach of Monaco Branding and Creative, explains three ways to establish trust.

Trust isn't fully established with one conversation, a single video, a quick email, or really any single event. Here are three "trust truths" that will help you build your personal brand:

Trust Truth 1: Engage Selflessly.
Customers will trust you when they feel like you are their number one advocate. Put yourself on their side. Relate.

Empathize. Understand. Make your customers feel more important than you are.

Trust Truth 2: Tune In and Listen.

This truth dovetails nicely with trust truth number one because paying attention via listening is a naturally selfless act. With a few strategically placed, prompting questions, you might get to know what deeply matters to your customer.

Trust Truth 3: Pursue Mindfully.

If the customer leans in for more, use discretion when you engage. The goal is to nurture, cultivate, and guide. Good salespeople, good marketers, and good branders will read the situation and gauge how much coaxing is required. Those who know when to push (and when not to push) win.

Think of trust-building like a time-release capsule. Provide small, sure, and steady doses of emotionally appropriate trust-building across every touch point of your customer's journey. The little wins you acquire will eventually add up to a bigger brand and sales.

NETWORKING

Networking is a tactic many people are uneasy doing. After all, who likes walking into a room of strangers? Here are some questions to ask yourself to enhance your networking skills, courtesy of Marie Zimenoff, CEO of Thought Leaders and Resumé Writing Academy.

Questions to ask yourself to improve your networking:

- How do you prefer to connect to your existing network?
- What have you done in the past to expand your network?
- What concerns stop you from taking actions to connect with or expand your network?
- How can you use your strengths to be more comfortable and effective in networking?

STORYTELLING

Part of reinvention is crafting a compelling story when you are pitching yourself on a sales call or a business meeting or networking. Here are five things to keep in mind from Precious Williams, the founder and CEO of Perfect Pitches by Precious, a media training, elevator pitches, sales, and branding company.

CREATING THE PERFECT POWER PITCH

1. **Timing is everything.** Keep your ideas clear, concise, and brief. A brilliant idea means nothing unless you can deliver it in a few moments of raw power. The more concise you can be, the more effective you will be. When you have written the content of your presentation, take the time to map out how it will be delivered. When practicing your presentation, attempt to replicate the actual delivery as closely as possible.

2. **Tell a story.** Storytelling is an essential aspect of sales pitches. It paints a picture of what life could be like

with your product. Use your story to dramatize, build engagement, and elicit emotional responses to seemingly emotionless objects and catch the attention of your audience.

3. **Be enthusiastic.** Pitching is about having the charisma, allure, and passion to get other people excited about what you're presenting. Be cautious not to take it overboard to the point where you seem arrogant. A good technique for increasing your energy level is to add about 50 percent more energy than you feel comfortable with.

4. **Be prepared for objections.** Understand that objections are usually nothing more than a mechanism that we use to get comfortable with what others are proposing before we agree with it. When people have an interest in what you are saying, they will certainly have questions. By formulating skillful and persuasive answers to these tough questions, it will help you demonstrate the array of abilities and traits that investors want to see.

5. **Offer a solution.** Your product may come with many wonderful features for customers to explore. Obviously, a lot of time and effort went into creating it. However, prospects are truly most interested in what your product can do for them. How exactly does your product solve their biggest problems? How much money will they save by using your product? And will using your product free up their time or improve their lives?

6. **Following up is critical.** Be consistent, reliable, and follow through on your word. Continue to follow up until you either get a yes or a definite no. Do not interpret a lack of response or any other kind of message as a no.

HEALTH AND WELLNESS

You can assist your reinvention and rebranding by ensuring you have a healthy lifestyle. Here are some facts to get you thinking about your own health and wellness, courtesy of Dr. Marion Recktenwald, founder of Thrive with Marion and Aging with Joy.

Did you know that:

- The World Health Organization (WHO) defines *health* as the state of complete physical, mental, and social well-being and not merely the absence of disease or infirmity.

- The United States is one of the wealthiest nations worldwide, but Americans have a shorter life expectancy compared with residents of almost all other high-income countries.

- A 2018 study showed that adherence to five low-risk lifestyle-related factors (never smoking, healthy weight maintenance, regular physical activity, healthy eating habits, and moderate alcohol consumption) could prolong life expectancy at age fifty years by 14.0 and 12.2 years for female and male US adults respectively compared with individuals who adopted zero low-risk lifestyle habits.

- Active longevity is 25 percent genes and 85 percent lifestyle choices.

- A healthy lifestyle can prevent 90 percent of US adults from getting Alzheimer's, and in the 10 percent with a strong genetic risk for cognitive decline, the disease can potentially be delayed by ten to fifteen years or more.

- Engaging in physical activity and not smoking topped the list of the WHO 2019 recommendations for lifestyle choices that will reduce the risks of developing dementia.

- Optimized and carefully targeted movement—when supported by other healthy lifestyle factors—can be the biggest blockbuster medication for body and brain at relatively low or no cost and without negative side effects.

* * *

This resource guide will be frequently updated and expanded on my website, Thrivingat50plus.com. Please check it out for more information, tips, and other assets.

ACKNOWLEDGMENTS

First, a special thank-you to Eric Koester (the founder of Creator Institute) for showing me I had this book inside me and providing the structure and support I needed to create it.

I could not have written this book without the generosity of the people I interviewed who opened their hearts and minds to me. I learned so much from what they shared of their reinvention and rebranding stories—and their insights. They have influenced my views of what it means to find purpose and meaning in your life at 50+. And they helped me find it within myself.

Specifically, I would like to thank the following people I interviewed:

William Arruda   Nancy Collamer
Nicolas Babin   Stacey Ross Cohen
Kim Norton Butler   Dorie Clark
Susan Chadick   Michael Drapkin

Suzy Drapkin	Jeff Sheehan
Richard Eisenberg	Jim Siegel
Judy Freedman	Sree Sreenivasan
Rita G.	Ray Stasieczko
Kerry Hannon	John Tarnoff
Naomi Kaufman	Patrice Tanaka
Keith Keller	Frederick G. Thompson
Evan Kirstel	Marie Zimenoff
Mitchell Levy	

Many thanks to the team at New Degree Press, especially
Linda Berardelli and Brian Bies, who believed in me and
helped me publish this book.

A special thank-you to Anne Lampert and Kathleen Becker
Blease for helping make me a better writer, to Laura Abbott
for her wickedly good editing eye, and to Arie Opzeeland
for his design skills.

For my friends and family who were there for me, and for
George for everything.

Thank you to the following people for their contributions to
make this book possible, and a special thank-you for Gerald
Ellenburg for being a superfan.

Lewis Abagnale	Drew Bartkiewicz
Rich Adler	Mathew Bergman
Laura Andreasen	Angela Bradley
Martin Arnold	Theresa Burnham

Joe Cafferelli
Cindy and John Cessna
Anita Connelly
Craig Copland
Andrew Corn
Chris Cosentino
Patty Costa
Dean Cyr
Vincent DePillo
Rebecca Denike
Elaine D'Andrea
Margot Einstein
Jill Ettinger-Diamond
Jerry Fallon
Valerie Foster
Alla Fridman
Frank Goushas
Art Green
Jeffrey Hoos
Alice Horncharik
Karen Howitt
Richard Imbruce
Barbara James
Richard Jones
Debbie Kelly
Gail Kushner
Julia Labaton
Henry Lee
Fran Lourie
Mitchell Lublin

Shelley Marx
George L. McGoldrick
George P. McGoldrick
Barry Miller
John Nardone
Deborah Nicolson
Kelmer Oldre
Robert Paolucci
Rich Papscoe
Anthony Petrocelli
Thomas A. Pick
Marion Recktenwald
Norman Roth
Peter Schelfhaudt
Margery J. Schneider
Joy Scott
David Seaman
Dennis Shiao
Lucy Siegel
Angelo Sisca
Bill Sobel
Lenore Sullivan
Sean Sullivan
Paul Timpanelli
Cathy Vitrella
Susan Wistrand
Zane Zumbahlen

APPENDIX

———

PREFACE
Agarwal, Dimple, Josh Bersin, Gaurav Lahiri, Jeff Schwartz, and Erica Volini. "The Longevity Dividend: Work in an Era of 100-Year Lives." *Deloitte Insights,* March 28, 2018. https://www2.deloitte.com/us/en/insights/focus/human-capital-trends/2018/advantages-implications-of-aging-workforce.html.

Schwartz, Jeff, Kelly Monahan, Steve Hatfield, and Siri Anderson. "No Time to Retire." *Deloitte Insights,* December 7, 2018. https://www2.deloitte.com/us/en/insights/focus/technology-and-the-future-of-work/redesigning-work-for-our-aging-workforce.html.

US Equal Employment Opportunity Commission. "EEOC Releases Fiscal Year 2018 Enforcement and Litigation Data. EEOC.gov. November 1, 2019. https://www.eeoc.gov/eeoc/newsroom/release/4-10-19.cfm.

INTRODUCTION
Clark, Dorie. "How to Reinvent Yourself After 50." *Harvard Business Review,* December 13, 2013. https://hbr.org/2013/12/how-to-reinvent-yourself-after-50.

Dweck, Carol S. "Growth Mindset: The Surprising Psychology of Self-Belief." NickWignall.com. Accessed on November 25, 2019. https://nickwignall.com/growth-mindset/

Freedman, Marc, "The Dangerous Myth of Reinvention." *Harvard Business Review.* https://hbr.org/2014/01/the-dangerous-myth-of-reinvention, January 1, 2014.

Hannon, Kerry. "The Key to Career Success After 50." *Forbes,* May 1, 2017. https://www.forbes.com/sites/nextavenue/2017/03/01/the-key-to-career-success-after-50/#5f69fea269f7.

Irving, Paul. "When No One Retires." *Harvard Business Review.*
https://hbr.org/cover-story/2018/11/when-no-one-retires, November 8, 2015.

Jenkins, Jo Ann, with Boe Workman. 2016. *Disrupt Aging: A Bold New Path to Living Your Best Life.* Public Affairs: New York, 2016.
https://www.aarp.org/entertainment/books/bookstore/money-work-retirement/info-2016/disrupt-aging-book.html.

Koehn, Nancy. 2011. "The Aging of American, as Opportunity." *The New York Times,* April 30, 2011.
https://www.nytimes.com/2011/05/01/business/01shelf.html

"Let's Retire Retirement." *Medium.* Accessed on November 28, 2019.
https://medium.com/@blackrock/lets-retire-retirement-a90976be5cc5

Lipnic, Victoria A. "The State of Age Discrimination and Older Workers in the US 50 Years After the Age Discrimination in Employment Act (ADEA)." *Eeoc.Gov,* June 2018.
https://www.eeoc.gov/eeoc/history/adea50th/report.cfm.

McLeod, Elizabeth, and Lisa Earle McLeod. "The Hidden Challenge to Getting Hired When You're Over 50—and How to Overcome It." *The Learning Blog,* May 2, 2018.
https://learning.linkedin.com/blog/advancing-your-career/the-hidden-challenge-to-getting-hired-when-your-over-50--and-howo.

Newport, Frank. "Snapshot: Average American Predicts Retirement Age of 66, Gallup. Accessed on November 15, 2019.

Schwartz, Jeff, Steve Hatfield, Kelly Monahan, and Siri Anderson, "No Time to Retire." *Deloitte Insights,* 2018.
https://www2.deloitte.com/us/en/insights/focus/technology-and-the-future-of-work/redesigning-work-for-our-aging-workforce.html.

Span, Paula. "Your Uber Driver Is 'Retired?' You Shouldn't Be Surprised," *New York Times,* October 25, 2019.
https://www.nytimes.com/2019/10/25/health/seniors-nontraditional-jobs.html.

CHAPTER 1

Barker, Eric. "6 Science-Backed Tips for Boosting Your Creativity," *The Week,* August 9, 2016.
https://theweek.com/articles/640778/6-sciencebacked-tips-boosting-creativity.

Clark, Amie. "Expert Interview Series: Kathy Gottberg: Aging and Living a Fulfilling Life." *The Senior List,* January 1, 2019. https://www.theseniorlist.com/blog/kathy-gottberg-aging-fulfilling-life/.

Dintino, Cecilia. "Growing Up Past 50," *Psychology Today.* April 17, 2019.
https://www.psychologytoday.com/intl/blog/midlife-matters/201904/growing-past-50?amp.

Dweck, Carol S. *Mindset: The New Psychology of Success.* Penguin Random House: New York, 2006.

Eisenberg, Richard. "New Mindset for Midlife Employees," Next Avenue, October 1, 2019. https://www.nextavenue.org/new-mindset-for-midlife-employees/.

"Encore Careers: Why an Aging Population Is a Resource, Not a Problem." Knowledge@Wharton. Accessed on July 4, 2019. https://knowledge.wharton.upenn. edu/article/encore-careers-why-an-aging-population-is-a-resource-not-a-problem/.

Freedman, Marc. *The Big Shift: Navigating the New Stage Beyond Midlife.* PublicAffairs: New York, 2011.

Gralla, Preston. "Old and in the Way." *Computerworld*, October 11, 2016. https://www.computerworld.com/article/3129428/old-and-in-the-way.html.

Green, Sarah."The Right Mindset for Success." *Harvard Business Review*, January 12, 2012. https://hbr.org/2012/01/the-right-mindset-for-success.

Hannon, Kerry. 2017. "The Key to Career Success After 50." *Forbes*, May 1, 2017. https://www.forbes.com/sites/nextavenue/2017/03/01/the-key-to-career-success-after-50/#5d82fca569f7.

Ibarra, Herminia. "How to Stay Stuck in the Wrong Career." *Harvard Business Review,* December 2002. https://hbr.org/2002/12/how-to-stay-stuck-in-the-wrong-career.

Oldford, Scott. "How to Upgrade Your Mindset and Defeat Your Biggest Obstacle as an Entrepreneur." *Entrepreneur,* March 20, 2018. https://www.entrepreneur.com/article/309496.

"Transtheoretical Model (or Stages of Change)—Health Behavior Change." Prochange.Com. Accessed on July 10, 2019. https://www.prochange.com/transtheoretical-model-of-behavior-change.

Vaynerchuk, Gary. "A Note to My 50-Year-Old Self | A Gary Vaynerchuk Original." YouTube. Accessed on November 16, 2019. https://www.youtube.com/watch?v=X7gcisj6KXA.

CHAPTER 2

Altucher, James. 2015. "The Ultimate Guide to Reinventing Yourself." *Medium.* Accessed on October 15, 2019. https://medium.com/the-mission/the-ultimate-guide-to-reinventing-yourself-1087afcb0e31.

Bennett, Roy T. 2017. "Change Begins at the End of Your Comfort Zone." *The Light in the Heart.* Accessed July 25, 2019. https://thelightintheheart.wordpress.com/2017/09/17/change-begins-at-the-end-of-your-comfort-zone-4/

"Chip Conley." *Travel Weekly*, August 6, 2018. http://travelweekly.texterity.com/travelweekly/august_6_2018/MobilePagedArticle. action?articleId=1415477#articleId1415477.

Condor, Bob. "Purpose in Life=Happiness." *Chicago Tribune,*
December 6, 2009, 2:00 a.m. CST.
https://www.chicagotribune.com/sns-health-life-purpose-happiness-story.html.

Craig, Nick, and Scott A. Snook "From Purpose to Impact."
Harvard Business Review., May 2014.
https://hbr.org/2014/05/from-purpose-to-impact.

Daum, Kevin. "5 Tips for Successful Reinvention." *Inc., May 2014.*
https://www.inc.com/kevin-daum/5-tips-for-successful-reinvention.html.

Dye, Lee. "Unemployment: UCLA Study Shows Stigma of Joblessness Is Immediate."
ABC News, April 5, 2011.
https://abcnews.go.com/Technology/unemployment-stigma-begins-quickly-makes-
job-search-harder/story?id=13302693.

Fry, Richard. "Baby Boomers Are Staying in the Labor Force at Rates Not Seen in
Generations for People Their Age." Pew Research Center. Accessed on October 15, 2019.
https://www.pewresearch.org/fact-tank/2019/07/24/baby-boomers-us-labor-force/.

Helgesen, Sally. "Helping Women Leaders Plot Their Next Career Move."
Strategy+Business, December 5, 2016.
https://www.strategy-business.com/blog/Helping-Women-Leaders-Plot-Their-Next-
Career-Move?gko=4bc2d.

Kamin Meyer, Tami. "You Can Reinvent Yourself, No Matter Your Age."
Next Avenue, January 15, 2019.
https://www.nextavenue.org/you-can-reinvent-yourself-no-matter-your-age/.

Leahy, Robert H. "Feeling Ashamed of Being Unemployed." *Psychology Today,*
October 9, 2013. 9.
https://www.psychologytoday.com/ie/blog/anxiety-files/201310/feeling-ashamed-
being-unemployed?amp.

Locker, Melissa. 2018. "Airbnb's Chip Conley Is Doubling Down on Being a 'Modern
Elder.'" *Fast Company,* October 23, 2018.
https://www.fastcompany.com/90255475/airbnbs-chip-conley-is-doubling-down-
on-being-a-modern-elder.

Oliver, Mary. 1990. *House of Light.* Boston: Beacon Press, 1990.

Rainey, Larissa. "The Search for Purpose in Life: An Exploration of Purpose, the
Search Process, and Purpose Anxiety." Master of Applied Positive Psychology
(MAPP)thesis, University of Pennsylvania, 2014. 60.
http://repository.upenn.edu/mapp_capstone/60.

Rohr, Richard. *Falling Upward.* San Francisco: Jossey-Bass, 2013.

Staats, Bradley R. 2018. *"Don't Just Dive Into Action: Stop to Think First."*
The Wall Street Journal, July 6, 2018.
https://www.wsj.com/articles/dont-just-dive-into-action-stop-to-think-first-1530888843

Stillman, Jessica. "Science Has Just Confirmed that If You're Not Outside Your Comfort Zone, You're Not Learning." *Inc., August 14, 2018.* https://www.inc.com/jessica-stillman/want-to-learn-faster-make-your-life-more-unpredictable.html.

Stulberg, Brad. "A Simple Equation Can Teach Us to Get Better Every Day." *Medium.* Accessed on October 1, 2019. https://medium.com/thrive-global/the-growth-equation-stress-rest-growth-de95a5cdcd1d.

"Success Isn't Comfortable: Lessons in Leadership from the Human Capital Institute." MIT Sloan Executive Education. Accessed on August 1, 2019. https://executive.mit.edu/blog/success-isnt-comfortable-lessons-in-leadership-from-the-human-capital-institute.

Webber, Rebecca. "Reinvent Yourself." *Psychology Today.* https://www.psychologytoday.com/us/articles/201405/reinvent-yourself, May 6, 2014.

CHAPTER 3

Daum, Kevin. 2014. "5 Tips for Successful Reinvention." *Inc., July 6, 2018.* https://www.inc.com/kevin-daum/5-tips-for-successful-reinvention.html.

Staats, Bradley. *Never Stop Learning.* " *Wall Street Journal,* July 6, 2018.

Webber, Rebecca. "Reinvent Yourself." *Psychology Today,* May 6, 2014. https://www.psychologytoday.com/us/articles/201405/reinvent-yourself.

CHAPTER 4

Craig, Nick, and Scott A. Snook. 2014. "From Purpose to Impact." *Harvard Business Review.* https://hbr.org/2014/05/from-purpose-to-impact, May 2014.

Condor, Bob. "Purpose in Life =Happiness." *Chicago Tribune,* December 6, 2009. https://www.chicagotribune.com/sns-health-life-purpose-happiness-story.html.

Oliver, Mary. *House of Light.* Boston: Beacon Press, 1990.

Rainey, Larissa. "The Search for Purpose in Life: An Exploration of Purpose, the Search Process, and Purpose Anxiety." Master of Applied Positive Psychology (MAPP)thesis, University of Pennsylvania, 2014. 60. http://repository.upenn.edu/mapp_capstone/60.

Rohr, Richard. *Falling Upward.* San Francisco: Jossey-Bass, 2013.

Sostrin, Jesse. 2018. "What to Do When Success Leaves You Empty." *Strategy+business,* April 16, 2018. https://www.strategy-business.com/blog/What-to-Do-When-Success-Leaves-You-Empty?gko=ec40d.

CHAPTER 5

Alboher, Marci. 2013. *The Encore Career Handbook*. New York: Workman Publishing, 2013.

Clark, Dorie. 2013. *Reinventing You: Define Your Brand, Imagine Your Future*. Boston: Harvard Business Review Press, 2013.

Collamer, Nancy. "5 Strategies for Reinventing Your Career," Better, Smarter, Richer. Accessed on September 1, 2019.

Dintino, Cecilia. "Re-Story Your Life." *Psychology Today*, January 29, 2016. https://www.psychologytoday.com/us/blog/midlife-matters/201801/re-story-your-life.

Gottschall, Jonathan. *The Storytelling Animal*. New York: Houghton Mifflin Harcourt, 2012.

Ibarra, Herminia, and Kent Lineback. "What's Your Story?" *Harvard Business Review*, January 2005. https://hbr.org/2005/01/whats-your-story.

Ibarra, Herminia. "How to Stay Stuck in the Wrong Career." *Harvard Business Review*, December 2002. https://hbr.org/2002/12/how-to-stay-stuck-in-the-wrong-career.

Rutledge, Pamela. 2011. "The Psychological Power of Storytelling." *Psychology Today*, January 16, 2001. https://www.psychologytoday.com/us/blog/positively-media/201101/the-psychological-power-storytelling.

CHAPTER 6

Brand Yourself. "51 Personal Branding Quotes: Powerful Advice You Can't Miss." Brand Yourself Blog. Accessed on September 5, 2019 https://brandyourself.com/blog/branding/personal-branding-quotes/.

Clark, Dorie. "How Women Can Develop—and Promote—Their Personal Brand." *Harvard Business Review,* March 2, 2018. https://hbr.org/2018/03/how-women-can-develop-and-promote-their-personal-brand.

Peters, Tom. "The Brand Called You." *Fast Company,* August 31, 1997. https://www.fastcompany.com/28905/brand-called-you.

Rogers, Anna. "What Are People Saying About Your Brand When You're Not in the Room?" Brands to Life, November 9, 2015. https://www.brandstolife.com.au/what-are-people-saying-about-your-brand-when-youre-not-in-the-room/.

Seymour, Lesley Jane. 2016. "The Joys of Losing Your Job in the Digital Age." LinkedIn. Accessed on September 5, 2019. https://www.linkedin.com/pulse/joys-losing-your-job-digital-age-lesley-jane-seymour/?trk=prof-post.

CHAPTER 7

Clark, Dorie. "How to Reinvent Yourself After 50." *Harvard Business Review,* December 13, 2013.
https://hbr.org/2013/12/how-to-reinvent-yourself-after-50.

Clark, Dorie. "Mentorship 2.0: How to Find the Mentor You Need," Porchlight Books Blog, Accessed on September 12, 2019.

Clark, Dorie. "Your Career Needs Many Mentors, Not Just One," *Harvard Business Review,* June 19, 2017.

Collamer, Nancy. "How Women Can Reinvent Their Careers After 50," Next Avenue, April 25, 2013.

Kerpen, Carrie. "Bringing Your Personal Brand to Life with Dorie Clark." *Inc.,* January 22, 2015.
https://www.inc.com/carrie-kerpen/bringing-your-personal-brand-to-life-with-dorie-clark.html.

Lumb, David. "Why You Need a Different Mentor at Every Step in Your Career." *Fast Company,* September 21, 2005.
https://www.fastcompany.com/3051253/why-you-need-a-different-mentor-at-every-step-in-your-career.

Meyer, Tami Kamin. "You Can Reinvent Yourself No Matter Your Age." Next Avenue, January 15, 2019.